NICOLE RICHIE

First published in Great Britain in 2011 by
TOPSPOT BOOKS
Suite 7, 40 Craven Street,
London WC2N 5NG

© **TOPSPOT 2011**

ISBN 978 1 905382 70 5

Cover Photo by Matt Baron/BEI/Rex Features:
2008 UNICEF Snowflake Lighting on Rodeo
Drive, Beverly Hills, Los Angeles, Nov 2008

All other images courtesy
REX FEATURES
and
Kadzen
Most Wanted
Charles Sykes
MB Pictures
David Fisher
Sipa Press
Jim Smeal/BEI
Sara Jaye
Matt Baron/BEI
BDG

INTRODUCTION

The days were when 'celebrity' wasn't a career choice. Not so very long ago, it was unrealistic to want to be famous when you grew up. It wasn't that fame itself was a bad thing, or even impossible. But even if it was unlikely for most people, fame wasn't an ends in its own right; it was something that came along the way, one of the trappings of success – just like getting paid well. Put another way, you were famous for something. Talent or achievement came first; fame came as a result.

Recently – perhaps just in the last fifteen or twenty years – that no longer holds true. The rise of Reality TV and the internet has seen a new phenomenon: the overnight celebrity. People can become famous, all over the globe, literally within a few hours. *Big Brother* is one of the best examples of this: a reality TV show that took regular, ordinary members of the public (at least, in its earlier series) and broadcast their every waking moment to the nation, turning them into country- and world-wide symbols of an instant-gratification culture. These examples proved it: you could be famous, millions of people could look up to you and follow your every move. And it could happen in a blink, without years of training or practice or hard work. It could even happen despite being otherwise totally ordinary.

That's the age we live in: when paupers can become kings and nobodies can become celebrities. The age-old American dream of making it for yourself, working your way up from rags to riches, got kicked up a notch. The sense is now that anyone can be a star: it just takes the right mixture of luck and opportunity.

Nicole Richie is possibly the ultimate example of this. She is insanely popular, particularly among the youth of California and America. And one of the reasons for that popularity is because she literally went from nothing to A-list star. She was born into what should have been a lifetime of obscurity, and possibly worse. Her parents weren't together, there was no hope of a happy, stable family for her. Even now, the identity of her biological mother is unknown to the public. But her mother did happen to work for someone whose eye the little Nicole caught, and he and his wife took her into their family and eventually adopted her. And it just so happened that he was a famous, multi-millionaire musician who could give her anything she wanted.

It could have been a fairytale ending, but happily-ever-after doesn't cut it any more. Fans love a rags-to-riches story; they also love conflict, and the threat of a riches-to-rags reversal. Privilege hadn't come without its price. Her parent's separation had left her with some major hang-ups. Her party lifestyle, culminating in a DUI charge after she was caught with drugs was nearly Nicole's undoing, but it also cemented her image in the popular press: this was someone who might have been handed life on a plate, but it wasn't going to be plain sailing for her.

That was the Nicole that millions watched and fell in love with on the first season of

The Simple Life. Post-rehab, she appeared wearing some fairly uninspiring clothes and a lot of extra pounds alongside Paris Hilton's sleeker, better-dressed model's body. The two girls ditzed their way through the series, showing their ineptitude and lack of life experience, but it was Nicole who came off better as the one with a little more self-awareness, that bit more capable of seeing herself from the outside. (The fact that Paris had become the subject of a media tsunami over her infamous sex tape probably helped the comparison.)

And so it was that she rose to fame, not because of any special talent, but almost because of what she wasn't. Described initially as Paris Hilton's 'chunky sidekick', there was no question of who the underdog was here. The public loved her all the same, and the producers came back to them for series after series.

That could have been it. Many celebrities of reality TV have been a temporary fixture; for every one of them who subsequently makes a career out of it, there are dozens who fall back into obscurity, never to be seen again. But Nicole managed to use the privileges of her background together with the publicity opportunity presented by *The Simple Life*, and recast herself. She lost weight, she restyled, and she made the most of the skills she already had but had never had a chance to air. 'She's not only dropped pounds, but also traded the coloured hair extensions and tacky minis and midriff-baring tops she once favoured for a more polished and sophisticated look,' wrote one magazine. 'As a result, she is now regarded as one of the most chic young women in the public eye.'

There followed a slew of new projects – books, fashion, singing – and a whole new life. But again, it wasn't to be the happy ending. A fall out with her best friend followed, along with problems with her weight and her health, and finally another DUI charge that threatened to put her behind bars for a year, derailing any hopes that her renewed image might be anything more than a blip. Once again, though, she managed to pick herself up, as she had in the past when drug and legal problems threatened to be her undoing.

And that's what it is about her that everyone loves. Even the cynics – especially the cynics – can see that the highs and lows of her life make great material. There is something compelling about her story, whether it's the car-crash television appeal of *The Simple Life* or the ups and downs of her day-to-day existence and relationships. As music producer Benny Medina once said, 'A celebutante in a fight with another celebutante, who socialises with the best of the best, who comes out of a drug addiction into an eating disorder – that's a lot of good copy. Now what do you want to do with it?' (Nicole herself has even recognised this and put it to good use, in a semi-autobiographical novel.)

Now in a new phase of her life, motherhood, Nicole has adapted once again and found a new role for herself. Her father, Lionel Richie, has commented on many occasions how proud he is of her, noting as a wry aside that he is also glad that her fame means she is spending her own money now, not his. Although her circumstances have changed, she is very capable of making the most of them at every turn. Nicole came to the public's attention as one of a pair of ditzy blondes, showing the world how inexperienced and sheltered they were. But now, it's becoming clearer than ever that she wasn't quite as clueless as the show's producers liked to make out.

1.

POOR LITTLE RICH GIRL

Nicole Richie was born in Berkeley, California, on September 21, 1981. In those earliest days, however, her association to the famous Richie family was a lot hazier. The name she was actually given at birth was Nicole Camille Escovedo. For a long time, her origins were fairly unclear – and to an extent, remain so. Her mother was an assistant to Lionel Richie, working backstage as the celebrated singer toured the country. Having first achieved global fame as the lead singer for the Commodores, the early 80s saw him launch a similarly successful solo career. Nicole was born in the period between these two phases of his life.

Nicole's father had long been rumoured to be Mexican-American musician and percussionist Peter Michael Escovedo, who was a member of

Richie's group – a backup drummer – at the time. In the past, Nicole has publicly denied this in at least some interviews. More recently, however, she has admitted that he is, in fact, her dad.

This had been a hot topic for some time on internet forums. For a while, Nicole's publicist would not tolerate any questions about her paternity. In 2004, though, Nicole herself decided to clear the matter up for good. The *Mail on Sunday* reported that Escovedo was indeed her father – her mother, on the other hand, has never been publicly identified.

'I know my parents, and what's hurt recently is that whole websites have sprung up talking about my heritage, whether I'm black or white. My parents were a mixture. I have French, Spanish, Indian and black. Even I don't know the whole mixture. And it doesn't matter. My birth parents both felt the Richies would provide a better life for me,' she told the Mail. 'I consider Lionel and Brenda to be my Mum and Dad.'

Lionel and his wife, Brenda, had noticed the little girl running around on their set and were entranced. The couple themselves did not have any children. Nicole's birth parents evidently weren't up to the job of taking care of her themselves – they did not remain together and apparently never considered themselves a couple. There was a solution there, and the Richies decided to suggest it. At the age of two, the little Nicole went to live with the famous singer and his wife.

At this stage, it was still a relatively informal arrangement. They would legally adopt her seven years later, when Nicole was nine, but for now things were fairly casual. Lionel Richie himself has given the impression that the whole thing was done on impulse. Certainly, the couple found out that parenting was a good deal harder than they had ever imagined. In fact, they didn't have a clue about how to look after a toddler.

The situation was evidently worse than they had ever expected. In fact, the Richies decided things were so bad that Nicole would benefit from weekly sessions with a psychotherapist – from the tender age of three. The therapy continued throughout her childhood.

In 1986 she started Kindergarten at the highly exclusive Buckley School in Sherman Oaks, California. Buckley boasts many famous alumni and the daughters of some of Hollywood's most notable, and it was here that she began her lifelong and bitter-sweet friendship with one Paris Hilton. The Buckley School's website states that, based on Dr Isabelle Buckley's experiences abroad, the school emphasises a well rounded program which focuses 'on academic training, physical development, moral education and creative expression.' Suffice to say that in the case of the two girls, it was partially successful. Nicole would later attend Montclair College Preparatory School, graduating in 1999, and the University of Arizona, where she studied Arts and Media.

It was at Buckley that she first tasted the attractions of fame. Recently she reported how two of her school friends formed a rap group called Caution, and how she wanted to get in on the act. 'I do love music and I did actually have my own band once,' she told *Absolute Now*. 'It was a rap band. I was eight and we were called Caution. It was my two friends, they called me and said, "We're in a band called Caution." And I was like, "Can I be in it?" So they made me audition! I had to sing down the phone even though we were a rap group. But they let me be in it. I really thought it was a big deal.' She even enlisted the help of her parents to give them a head start in their new career. 'All I can think of is the three of us going up to my mom and singing her our first song. We were dead serious. And I even remember part of our rap. The rap lyrics I remember were: "Caution! Walking down the street./You better watch out, and step to the beat/Playing our music from town to town/Rockin' and Rollin' were gonna get down!" My poor mom had to sit there with a straight face and watch us perform. We asked her to find us a manager,' she said.

Nicole's well-publicised childhood was by no means smooth. For starters, her parents were often away. Nicole learned to believe that was normal. 'I just knew that he wasn't gonna be there,' she told Oprah. 'If I had a recital I wasn't like, "Oh, my God, I hope that my dad's gonna come." I was just thinking to myself, "OK, I have a recital and my dad will call and he'll ask me how it was. And that's my life – and that's how every child grows up." My mom definitely was more there, but, at the same time, she was trying to lead a life as well. A lot of time she would go with him.'

Keeping the company they did meant that the little Nicole gained a lot of attention from time to time, though little of it was regular contact with anyone who could be called a role model. The Richies and their wealthy friends compensated for this deficiency with money. Kenny Rogers once bought Nicole a white mini-Mercedes for Christmas. She was four at the time. She has spoken about her wild spending trips to jewellers, before she was even old enough to know what she was buying. Fabergé eggs were one of her favourites. 'I didn't know what they were, but I knew they were cute and my mum liked them. So I would go to Gearys and charge them. At the end of the year Dad got the bill and I've never had a charge account there since. I was eight.'

Although her birth parents were right, and life in the Richie household offered financial advantages beyond what they could ever offer her, it also had its serious downsides. All was not well between Lionel and Brenda. The relationship was breaking down, and the situation brought out the worst in them. At times, it could even turn violent. The media loved this, which was torture to Lionel, who just wanted to keep his personal life out of the spotlight. Unfortunately, that wasn't possible when the police had to be involved.

In 1988, there was a nasty incident involving Lionel, Brenda and a woman called Diane Alexander, who Lionel was dating and would later marry. Evidently, Brenda took exception to the competition – despite the fact that they had long since parted ways formally – and ended up punching and kicking both her husband and Diane. 'Once the police came for the disturbance, that's when it became a mess,' he told *Jet*. 'One thing people don't realize is that long before that happened, Brenda and I were separated. We were not living in the same house. All you read about was that Lionel got caught. I hadn't told the press that we were separated. When I finished my Dancing on the Ceiling tour, I came home and moved out.'

The press spun it their own way, saying that he had been beaten up by a woman and calling him a 'wuss'. 'I said to one member of the press, "Let me ask you a question: Would you have liked it the other way if it was said 'Lionel Richie Beat Up His Wife?' Does that sound better?" The guy said "no." Then I said when a couple has an argument and it gets physical, wouldn't most guys just not throw a punch at all? I didn't do anything to Brenda. And that sounds better than I knocked her out.'

The separation hit Nicole hard – and that hit the Richies hard, too. Lionel has often spoke of feeling guilty about they way it affected his daughter, and how he and his ex-wife indulged her every desire as a result. Even before the problems started, however, Nicole's childhood was far from ideal. For all the Richies' fame and money, there was little time to spend with them – even when she did go away with them. 'I was always going on tour with Dad,' she said. 'He wasn't particularly into sex, drugs and rock 'n' roll, but there were certainly people around him who were. I never realised it was anything out of the ordinary. My best friend at the time was Kimberly.' This was the daughter of Rod Stewart, whose career was enjoying highs similar to Lionel's at the time. 'Rod was always on tour, and she would go with him. I thought that was the way every child grew up. I thought every little girl had a rock star daddy.'

One of the problems was that Lionel didn't

see himself as a rock star yet. He was famous because he used to be a Commodore, not in his own right as a solo performer. So he began working even harder. 'And I wasn't focusing at all on what Nicole was doing but where do I go next with "Hello" or "All Night Long,"' he admitted. 'I wasn't there.'

Lionel found that the late hours and long trips he put in gained him the success he wanted, but like many celebrity parents he realised – too late – that his fame came at a price. 'If you look back on my career, it's one of those situations where you have to ask, "Am I winning or am I losing?"' he told *Jet*. 'Okay, I've got hit records. I'm famous around the world. I'm comfortable in my living. Then you start asking the questions, "But was I there for my kid during the recitals? Was I there for my kid's graduation? Was I there?" And a lot of the times the answer was, especially in Nicole's case, no... I was trying my best at that time to be Lionel Richie. I wasn't Lionel Richie yet. I was an ex-Commodore.'

Her parents' separation, so soon after they had formally adopted her, was extremely tough. 'When my dad divorced my mom it was kind of like him leaving me also. I just really didn't understand why he wasn't returning my phone calls, or why I couldn't see him whenever I wanted to. That was the most hurtful thing to me,' she said. She left Lionel's household to live with Brenda after the break-up, and has described how her mother was in such a bad state that she ended up having to take care of her. In the past, she has put a positive spin on what had been a terrible situation for them. 'She was devastated like any person would be. But it was a good thing that I took care of my mom because I didn't really get a chance to get that upset because I was wanting to make everyone happy.' Lionel has Nicole to thank for her efforts, since she is responsible for keeping them on speaking terms – at least in the long run. 'I have a great relationship with Brenda now. Nicole has done a great job keeping us in tune with each other.'

But whilst she was propping up Brenda, Nicole herself was storing up problems for her own future crisis. This is a frequent feature of childhoods – particularly celebrity childhoods – where the child in question is forced to grow up too fast. Sooner or later, their lost years catch up with them.

It started with relatively normal and benign things, like lying to her parents about which of their houses she was sleeping at, and then going off to a friend's house instead. 'I was very good at manipulating my parents because they were getting a divorce and they didn't speak to each other and I really used that to my advantage. I would call my mom and say I was going to my dad's or, you know, call my dad and say I was going to my mom's and I knew that they wouldn't call each other.' She'd mix her outfits up – grunge rock and hippie being two favourites – and dye her hair green. But in Nicole's case, the troubles also manifested themselves in some fairly serious teenage rebellion and drug use.

'I had the freedom to do what I wanted. My dad wasn't really around and my mom was just doing her thing. When you're a girl and 13, you're at a rebellious stage anyway. And I definitely wasn't listening to my parents anyway. From the time I was 9 through 13, nobody was around. So, when they did start coming around, they started telling me what to do.' It was too late by then; at 14 she was getting into Hollywood clubs with a fake ID, and not long afterwards smoking and drinking heavily. 'I can't say exactly when it started but I experimented with everything,' she said. 'I am not proud of what I did. Being in Beverly Hills puts certain pressures on you, but so does being a teenager anywhere. You want to fit in. You want to be part of the crowd. You want to experiment. So you smoke, you drink and you do drugs.'

She has shown a surprising lack of insight about all this, for a girl who has been through so much therapy. 'There are a few questions people always ask me that I still don't have answers to,' she told *Cosmo Girl*. 'They want to know why I started drinking and doing drugs when I was 13 – what the deeper meaning behind it was. Part of the reason a lot of people do drugs is to hide feeling bad. For me, though, it wasn't about escaping family issues or boy problems – I've always had really close relationships with my family' – something her father would no doubt disagree with. 'I think there's a lot of reasons,' she later said of her drug abuse. 'I think that, yes, my parents were going through a lot. I think it also just had to do with me and my personality and me wanting to kind of be free. I mean I constantly had security guards around me when I was younger and I wasn't allowed to go to the mall with a lot of my friends and stuff like that. And so, when I finally was able to sneak out, I would just really, really take it to the next level.'

There was, she admits, one common way of rebelling that she did not take. 'I've been careful to never let boys cause trouble for me – I was a virgin until I fell in love at 19, because I never wanted to give anyone a reason to start rumours about me. So I guess I just started partying to change things up. To get out of feeling anything.'

Friends with Paris Hilton since she was two years old, and as the pair went to the Buckley School together, it is unsurprising that some of her misdemeanours also involved the blonde celebrity heiress. 'We were just like sisters from the moment we met,' she told *Harper's Bazaar*. 'Once, when we were 12 or 13 and we were in Vegas, we went on the Strip with our friends from high school. We were walking around and we couldn't get a cab, so we saw some cops and asked, "Hi, can we have a ride home?" They said, "How old are you?" and we said, "Eighteen." My parents got a call saying, "Paris and Nicole are out on the streets."'

With Lindsay Lohan at the 13th Annual Race To Erase Ms Benefit For The Nancy Davis Foundation For Multiple Sclerosis, Century City, US, May 2006

She has claimed that her parents were not to blame for any of her childhood problems, and that she would have rebelled without their turbulent separation. 'I was someone who was always going to get into trouble.' Lionel Richie is under no illusions, though, and has admitted responsibility for her wild years in the past – notably on Oprah, where he and Nicole openly discussed their relationship and the problems of the past.

Nicole started on soft drugs when she was 13 but rapidly graduated to the hardest stuff. 'Being a teenager and a girl in Hollywood is tough,' she explained to the *Daily Mail*. 'You feel like you want to be older. It sounds crazy, but I feel lucky because a lot of my friends were going through drug and drink problems at the same time as me. It was like a bonding process.' It began with marijuana, but by 14 she was taking cocaine, and then the prescription drugs Valium and Xanax, an anti-anxiety drug. But the problems really started when she tried heroin. She was addicted straight away.

'Heroin makes you not care about anything,' she told the *New York Times*. 'It makes you very oblivious, and you're down all the time, and that worked for me. I look back at pictures and my skin was grey, my nails had gunk in them, and I didn't even notice.' Her father obviously noticed something was going on, though he was more concerned about her driving – full licences are issued as young as 16 in California. 'When Nicole got to driving age, those were the hair-raising years,' he told the Mail. 'I remember the nights when, if the phone rang at 2am, I'd get nervous. Or when the door slams in the night and I'd think, "She's in, thank God. I can go to sleep." Any parent understands those feelings – it's the same all over the world. Except in Hollywood, it's the hippest of the hip, the hottest of the hot. The labels, the clubs. All of that. Nicole was floundering; she had big challenges. When you're adopted, sooner or later you ask, "Who am I; where do I fit in?" It was a truly terrible time.'

After graduating from high school she attended the University of Arizona, where she studied Arts and Media. She didn't finish the course. 'I stopped because I went there for two years and I felt like I experienced college or whatever,' she explained. 'I'm over it. I like Hollywood better.'

As luck would have it, her best friend Paris Hilton would open a new door for her. Fox Television were looking to break new ground in the field of comedy, and they had realised that Paris was a great way to go about it. The brief was to create a comedy programme, but outside of the standard sitcom format that, the executives felt, had grown tired over the years.

For their inspiration, they chose *Green Acres*, a classic 1960s sitcom. The premise was simple: a wealthy New York lawyer who has always hankered after country living drags his unwilling socialite wife away from the comforts of the city to a run-down farm, which he has purchased from a con man. The two struggle to do the place up and adapt to life away from their normal creature comforts. The show ran to six series.

Fox decided that this would be a perfect idea to adapt to reality television. All they needed were a couple of wealthy, sheltered, air-headed young girls who had never wanted for anything in their lives and never had to take a low-paying manual job – especially one on a farm – and throw them head first into rural life. It was Fox's first foray into the field of reality TV, so it had to be good. 'We're really committed to scripted programming and it's going to be the vast majority of what we do,' said the company's co-president. 'That being said, we are part of a company that is as big a content provider as there is. When a great idea comes up from someone inside our division, we're going to pursue it whether it is scripted or unscripted or something else altogether.' There would be high expectations for the show.

The first character they cast was easy enough. Paris Hilton, hotel heiress and model, got the job. Strangely, the casting director claimed not to pick her for her obvious ineptitude with all things country. 'I'm used to meeting with actors who are putting on a facade,' said Sharon Klein. 'She was so real. She was funny. At that first meeting she did not come off stupid. She was in her own reality and not embarrassed to talk about it. There was a sweetness to her.' For a while, Nicky Hilton, Paris's sister, was slated to do the show with her, but – unlike Paris – she preferred to stay out of the limelight. Paris suggested that she should do the show alone, but the studio execs were adamant that it should be a pair. Paris supposedly asked several of her friends to take part, but in the end the agreement was made with Nicole. It was an answer to her childhood dream of being famous, like her platinum-selling father.

Lionel himself saw this as an altogether different kind of fame, and one that wouldn't do the Richie family name any favours. He himself had come in for some harsh words from his father when he decided to become a singer, and was almost as horrified about Nicole. 'I was not thrilled. You wouldn't be able to print what my father said when I wanted to play in the Commodores and I said the same words to my daughter when she explained that she was going to ruin the family name with a TV show,' *Contactmusic* quoted him. 'There's Paris and Nicole in my living room talking about this wonderful reality TV they're going to make, and my stomach leaps out the window.'

'Paris suggested they should contact me,' Nicole told the *Mail on Sunday*. 'I'd been approached by other reality-TV shows, but all they wanted to do was the "rich bitch" thing – to follow me around shopping. I do go shopping, but there's a lot more to me than just flexing a credit card.'

If she was hoping to show what a balanced,

rounded individual she was, she would be disappointed. But there was another minor problem to navigate first: Nicole was hopelessly hooked on smack and that really wasn't conducive to do anything constructive, let alone performing for the cameras for hours at a time. 'I knew I could not go on television being as wasted as I was,' she later admitted. So it was that, before she started her new life living on a farm for a month amongst the good rural folk of Altus, Arkansas, that she took a similar amount of time out to clean up in rehab.

In an interview with CosmoGirl, she spoke about how she made the transition from being a party girl to realising that there was something she needed to fix. 'I've always loved having fun and being like "la la la." And I was like that when I was staying out all night partying with my friends. But then I reached a point when I knew I couldn't go on living the kind of life where I woke up each morning wondering, "Oh God, what did I do last night?" What kind of trouble am I going to get in? I started looking at my life and the people I was hanging out with. Friends of mine were dying – not from overdosing, but in car accidents. It was just really dark. My dad had even become wary of letting me hang out with my brother and sister. And I missed them. I just wanted to be close with my family and I just wanted to be healthy.'

Her relationship with her father had always been close, but her situation was now threatening that. 'I'm not one to hide things from my parents. So I had no problem going up to my dad and being like, "Listen, this is what's going on, and I need help." He knew – everyone knew – but they also knew that the only way I was going to be helped was by seeking out help myself. He and my mom and everyone around me were very supportive, like they'd been waiting for me to say it for a while. And so my parents and I made a decision to check me in for rehab at Sierra Tucson, in Tucson, Arizona.

'I was in such a messed-up state when I got to rehab that I didn't really think about what I was getting into. And in my reality, so many people I knew had been through rehab that it wasn't a big deal. We did a lot of group therapy and work with horses. I made strong friendships there – you become close to people when you're helping each other.'

The time spent breaking the grip the drug

had on her wasn't entirely voluntary. In fact, there was the awkward matter of a DUI charge – something she claims was monumentally unlucky, since she had already resolved to go into rehab, and even set a date. In February 2003 – just three months before production on *The Simple Life* was about to start – she was pulled over by police whilst driving her Mercedes in California. She admitted driving with a suspended licence. Unfortunately, however, they had the foresight to rummage around a bit more, and happened to stumble across a quantity of dirty white powder.

'Well, actually the day that I decided that I wanted to go and we had picked the day to go to rehab I had a week in between that day and when I actually went,' she explained. 'So, that day that I was driving was actually like the one time I wasn't doing anything wrong and I wasn't even driving my car. I was driving a friend's car. And I got pulled over for I think it was bad tags or something like that... It was just a traffic stop for bad tags and when the cop came to the car they had found a balloon of heroin on the floor of the passenger seat and – and I had begged and pleaded and said that it wasn't mine. And, you know, you can always tell,' she continued, describing the ethical dilemma the cops found themselves in. 'You can look at someone's eyes and tell if they are sober or not and they knew that I was – that I was fine, but at the same time I am driving a car and the car had drugs in it, so technically I have to go to jail for it. And, the first thing I thought was, what am I going to do? I can't tell my parents. I absolutely can't tell my parents. And I just really wanted to get out at that point.'

Her father, who had long known that his daughter had problems, was relieved more than anything else – though he maintained at the time that she was just carrying it for a friend. 'It was in her car but it didn't belong to her; she wasn't doing heroin...' *The Simple Life* might have been a disaster for their reputation, but he knew it was going to be a great motivator for getting her clean.

'The day she came to me and said, "Dad, I have a problem," it was a breakthrough,' he told the *New York Times*. 'It was partly because she wanted to do *The Simple Life* so badly, she knew she'd have to get herself straight for it.' Nicole was mandated into rehab by the court; the sentence on the drug charge was deferred, and she had to appear back in court to give a progress report just three days before filming began. 'I give her a lot of credit for that. I was just so relieved when she realised that maybe she was going too fast down the road. I'm so proud of her. She made it through the tunnel.' Her father took a fortnight off to spend time with her and help her through it.

'The first few days actually I don't necessarily remember just because they were so horrible,' she told CNN. But, you know, I mean you get really sick and it's scary when I think back on – on how physically ill I was just because I did not have everything in me that I – that I used to have in me. And the fact that I was taking something that was so powerful that I became physically addicted to it is really scary and, you know, I mean it was just – it was really bad. And then by the end of the 30 days, they take a picture of you when you walk in and then they take a picture of you when you leave and the change was just really out of control.'

Chief amongst Nicole's issues to work through in therapy was her abandonment issues. These had largely been prompted by Lionel's affair when she was eight; this, of course, had been splashed across the media in the most public way, and had resulted in Nicole moving away from her father to live with Brenda. 'Both of my parents came for a family week, and we all sat in a room, which has never happened, and we discussed everything,' she said. 'A bunch of feelings came up that I didn't even know that I had because I was so used to numbing myself.'

Rehab seemed to work. 'When Nicole came out of the programme, she was so clear as to who she was and where she wanted to go,' Lionel said. 'At about 22, I could have a conversation with her that made sense. And you know what? Nicole's rehab saved my life and my sanity, too. For a guy who doesn't have addictions, I learned more from those two weeks than anything else I've ever experienced in my life. We went through it as a family, and the opening line really got me. This guy asked, "How many of you are here to save your loved ones?" The appropriate thing is to raise your hand, of course. But then he said, "You're not here to save them. They're here to save themselves. You're here to save you." Ah!' Perhaps unsurprisingly, having the impetus to take time off in favour of spending it with his daughter – not something he would have done without a major push – brought

Lionel and Nicole closer together.

Nicole genuinely seems to have believed that this ended her drug problems. A year later, she told *Jet*, 'I'm really lucky because a lot of people don't get over it until they're in their 40s.' And she agreed with Lionel that it had drawn them together. 'We're really, really close and we weren't at all before.' Lionel also admitted that he had learned from his mistakes with Nicole; he had made sure to carve out time for the children from his next marriage. 'I want to make as many memories for them as I can. And Nicole is a great big sister for them. I know now that the key word in family is "communicate." Communicate, communicate, communicate!'

Lionel's own personal life hadn't been great over the last few months, so it's understandable that he had let things slip with Nicole. At around the same time that she was picking up a DUI charge, his marriage was on the rocks and he was headed for divorce. At least for him, it was all inspiration. 'I started out with this album writing songs like Just For You, I Still Believe and One World and I was going in a very positive direction. I wrote She's Amazing with a wonderful artist called Seven. I collaborated with Lenny Kravitz and that was amazing. Then, all of a sudden, my marriage fell apart.' Having married Diane Alexander in 1995, soon after his break from Brenda, the pair ended up divorcing in January 2004. 'It's hard to lie to yourself when you're feeling certain things personally. I found myself writing Ball and Chain and these other songs based on sheer emotion. The album got more and more honest as it kept going along. By the time I ended this album, it was a pure album that came straight from the heart.'

After the highs and lows of the last 20 years, he says he took away one important lesson. 'Career is wonderful, but at the end of my journey, family is going to be the only thing in that room with me. And I want to make sure that I'm worthy of their being there.' In fact, this was something that Nicole had helped him to understand in more than one way. Although he was going through the mill with his latest separation, a silver lining came in the form of a renewed friendship with his ex-wife, Brenda. The two had been on shaky terms since the acrimonious separation in 1988, and subsequent divorce proceedings. But now, with the three forced to share a therapist's couch over the fortnight-long course of Nicole's rehab, they began to repair the rift – the common interest being their daughter's wellbeing. 'I think I was 20 when they started talking. And they actually didn't start talking until I went to rehab. Now they're best friends. And it's really great,' the *Daily Express* quoted her.

For years after that, Nicole was careful when talking about her sobriety (drug addicts and alcoholics are fond of counting days, months and years sober) because she knew the temptations. 'Part of the reason I don't really want to talk about being sober is that I don't want to feel the pressure of being a role model. I am learning so much about myself that for me to tell other people what to do in their lives is something I am not really fit to do. I am a work in progress, I am not there yet,' she told Harper's Bazaar. 'I don't know whether I will ever be there.'

Nicole Richie out and about, Los Angeles, Jun 2010

*Joey And T
Fashion Show,
Mercedes Benz
Fashion Week,
LA, Oct 2003*

2.
A SIMPLE LIFE?

When Nicole was clean and sober, they went to work on *The Simple Life*. The show wasn't just about throwing a couple of privileged rich girls into farm life and watching them deal with it – like a kind of Beverly Hillbillies in reverse. It was a little more shaped than that to take best advantage of the material. 'There's a structure to storytelling in scripted programming that we tried as much as we could to impose on how we told the stories of what went on there,' said Brad Johnson, senior VP of comedy development at Fox. 'It's a way of storytelling that isn't just random slice of life. We worked with our editors and producers to impose a little bit of comedic editing and structure.'

So it was that they moved to a pig farm in Altus, a village with a population of 800. Naturally, they weren't provided with regular farm-wear; Manolo Blahniks were the order of the day, not green wellies. But it wasn't all mud and muck; aside from the film crew that accompanied them 24/7, they got to bring Tinkerbell with them – Paris's Chihuahua. The rest is history. When the show was aired a few months later, millions tuned in to watch.

Of course, Nicole's drug and family-related problems weren't the only things that threatened to get in the way of her beckoning fame as the co-star of a reality TV show. There was also the matter of her friend's indiscretions – which, thanks to the marvel of the internet, were being uncontrollably broadcast around the world. The incident itself had taken place in 2001, but the powers that be had held onto the amateur footage until now. Shortly before *The Simple Life* débuted, Paris Hilton appeared in all her glory across the internet.

The 55-minute-long film showed the 19-year-old Paris Hilton with her boyfriend at the time, Rick Salomon – *Beverley Hills 90210* actress Shannon Doherty's separated husband – in the throes of passion, occasionally stopping to reposition herself for the benefit of the camera and, presumably, whatever audience she had originally intended.

As soon as the video came to light, Paris went silent. She stopped doing publicity for the show and went into hiding. All interviews were refused. Salomon denied being the origin of the tape's leak, but it didn't matter by then. The damage was done – initially to Paris's reputation, which would never be the same again, but also, the Fox exec's feared, to the reputation of their station and programme. 'It's been a difficult time for her,' said Nicole. 'But we all make mistakes. This will blow over like everything blows over.'

Salomon had timed the release for maximum effect. It caused a media storm that threatened to overshadow Fox's new project. Paris tried denial at first. 'He's a complete liar and scumbag,' she told New York Magazine, when rumours of the film's existence started circulating. 'He is a very sick man. People love to talk shit because they're jealous. I don't care. Whatever.' Unfortunately, she couldn't deny that the film existed when it spread across the Internet. Neither could the Hilton family influence buy her out of trouble; despite the threat of legal action, the downloads rolled on. They finally settled for a statement, 'The Hilton family is greatly saddened at how low human beings will stoop to exploit their daughter, Paris, who is sweet-natured, for their own self-promotion as well as profit motives.'

She tried suggesting that she was 'out of it', hadn't known what she was doing when the film was made, and hadn't approved its release, but Salomon sued her for defamation. She counter-sued, and ended up settling out of court. Some sources suggest that she received $400,000. In a later interview with *GQ*, however, she claimed, 'I never received a dime from the video. It's just dirty money and he should give it all to some charity for the sexually abused or something. I mean I so did it for attention, but still...'

Things weren't great for Paris, but *The Simple Life* also threw Nicole into the spotlight in a way that she had never experienced before. The show scored more than 16 million viewers, turning it into America's third highest-rated show. The reviews were as tongue-in-cheek at best, but tended to admit that the show's creators had known what they were doing.

'An updated "*Green Acres*," the show distills the most disturbing elements of existing reality shows – the voyeurism of "The Real World," the gross-out antics of "Fear Factor" and the sexual humiliations of "The Bachelor." Yet by some strange twist of television alchemy "*The Simple Life*" is not nearly as mean-spirited,' commented the *New York Times*. 'The mockery is overt and good-natured, a "Cold Comfort Farm" for the MTV generation.

'The beauty of the casting is that the two young women do not have to strain very hard to fit their assigned roles,' the reviewer continued, in a decidedly back-handed compliment. 'Nicole is perkier and better mannered; she smiles a lot and thanks her hosts repeatedly. Paris, platinum blond and alarmingly thin, appears to have almost no affect. She struts about the farm with the blank hauteur of an Eastern European runway model. Her descriptive powers are delightfully limited. As the two struggle to herd cows or pour fresh milk into bottles, she moans in her flat, monied drawl, "I'm going to die."

'Viewers are supposed to laugh at the harebrained heiresses in their high-heeled shoes and Von Dutch baseball hats, but not too harshly; these days relatively few Americans of any age or background have much experience hand-plucking chickens or milking cows. The promos suggest that the "Simple Life" reality was molded to conform to a storybook arc: as time passes, the girls end up performing barn chores that might make a grown lawyer faint.'

Viewers noted that, although both girls were shallow, materialistic and self-centred, Nicole somehow managed to come off better than her co-star. 'Paris Hilton spent the entire time on the farm remarking (apparently surprised): "Eeuw... this stinks." Richie, who had just come out of rehab for a raging heroin addiction, was much the same as Paris, but somehow very likeable as well,' wrote the Mail's reviewer. Part of the reason for this was her sense of humour, and ability to look at herself – at least occasionally – with something approaching objectivity. 'She was sassy, and sometimes actually intentionally funny. "I am not plucking anything but my eyebrows," she deadpanned, when faced with a chicken which required de-feathering. And so Richie was, surprisingly, taken to the bosom of middle America. While Paris was often sulky and silent, Nicole Richie was warmer and wittier.'

What with one thing and another, Nicole wasn't used to all the new attention. In her own words, she admitted that 'things have gone haywire.' Uncharitable reviewers dubbed her 'Nouveau Richie' and a 'Celebutante'. And aside from the show itself – which prompted questions that she was just a rich girl from a privileged family, with no talent of her own – there was the scandal around Paris's ill-judged film début, and the trial of her godfather Michael Jackson on child molestation charges, in which she defended the star.

'I hugged him and he thanked me for sticking by him,' she said, after attending a support rally for the singer at Neverland Ranch. However, not long afterwards, when *The Simple Life* had made her own life considerably less simple, she found herself giving more considered, public-image-aware commentary. 'It is important to let the law do what it has to do,' she told the *Sunday Mail*.

'But if there is a jury trial then I can't see how it will be fair. I've known Michael all my life and there is no one like him. I've stayed at Neverland many times as a child, both with my parents and without. I have slept over. He's strange and different, but just because someone dyes their skin and grows their hair, that doesn't make them a child molester. He has never laid a finger on me.'

She went so far as to defend him on CNN, and said that in all the times she had stayed over with her friends, nothing untoward had happened. 'You know, a group of us would all sleep in the same room,' the *New York Beacon* quoted her. 'It was like, absolutely nothing more than just... an adult kind of wanting to be a kid again. Just, you know, enjoying the company of children. I grew up with him. I have spent many evenings there and many days there, and I can only speak for myself. I will say that absolutely nothing went on.' She also made it clear that she would have spoken up if she had had any doubts. 'I'm not a quiet person. If there was something going on, I'd be like "who are you?"... and I'd tell my parents. But my parents would never put me in hands that they thought were dangerous. I never had any complaints, and you know, I love him.'

'But I would really question a mother who allows her child to sleep over with a 43-year-old man,' she qualified her support. 'I'm not saying this child deserved it, but I wouldn't let my child stay with someone who had been accused of child molestation before. The whole world is judging Michael right now. If he's acting weird, who can blame him?'

Her life wasn't under much less scrutiny, though it wasn't as harsh as Jackson's press. 'People are always trying to take digs at me,' she told the *Mail on Sunday* in an interview during a lull in the storm that had become her life. 'I am not sure why, but if I let every criticism hurt me, I'd have given up a long time ago. I guess I'm developing a thick skin. I'm not trying to make out I'm a genius, but, with me, what you see is what you get. I'm proud of what I've accomplished and I'm proud of how far I've come in my personal life. What I do isn't rocket science, but nor should people dismiss me as an airhead. You don't get to where I am by being dumb.'

Although she had always been a part of the rich and famous clique, fame itself had been something that had actually eluded her. When it came along, it was rather a surprise. 'You have to understand, I come from a privileged background. I grew up in Los Angeles and all my friends, such as Paris and Kimberley were from rich, famous families and so I thought nothing of it. I never realised that being rich and famous was anything unusual. Then it all changed.'

'I can't complain, but it's been one hell of a roller-coaster ride,' she claimed. 'Suddenly, everything I did was open to scrutiny.' Not only what she did, but who she was: being thrust into the limelight also saw a spotlight shone on her own parentage. Online forums around the world were overrun with speculation about her biological mother and father at the time, and the topic soon became one that her publicist desperately sought to avoid. There were also questions about her drug-taking and arrest, which she did her best to put in a positive light.

'I've sorted myself out now. Last year was the worst and the best of years. Going to rehab was tough, but I feel grateful that I sorted myself out before the whole fame thing hit. I like dealing with life clean and sober. God knows what I'd be like if I was still using drugs. I feel like I can cope with things now.' She explained her indiscretion by blaming Cher – a celebrity who has admitted some sparing drug use in the 1970s, but who claims she was terrified of the harder stuff. 'I went to a Cher concert when I was a child, and she told the crowd to experiment and do things when you're young because it's so much less dignified to do drugs and drink when you're older. But I've done my partying, and I feel like I'm growing up.' Although her friendship group was formerly part of the problem, since they were all doing it, she claimed that they were now all on the straight and narrow. 'These days I go out with a clean, sober crowd. We've all been through rehab.' In other words, she was setting herself up for a fall.

Although she was open about her drug use and rehab, there were still some areas of life that she considered off-limits to the press. 'I don't want to talk about boyfriends,' she said. Having dated Tobey Maguire of *Spider-Man* fame, she was clearly of interest to the gossip mags. But, she maintained, 'There are some things that have to stay private, no matter who you are. That's the biggest lesson I've learned from all this publicity.' However much was different in her life, though, she admitted that some things would always stay the same. 'I have changed and I'm growing up, but I still like to have a bit of retail therapy. The only difference these days is the money I'm spending is my own.'

Nicole Richie out and about, with DJ Am, 2005

The Simple Life didn't just push the two girls – along with their respective indiscretions – into the spotlight. Lionel Richie also found himself the subject of renewed attention, something that he wasn't happy about either, especially since his second wife was in the process of taking him to the cleaners. One of the biggest headlines appeared when it became known that Diane was demanding $300,000 per month in living expenses. 'When I saw those numbers, I called up my accountant and asked, "How much did you say I have, because $300,000 a month means I'm making about a billion,"' he told *JET*. The second time around, though, he claims that the reconciliation process was a lot quicker. 'With Diane, I must tell you we are healing very, very nicely. What has happened, for the most part, is sometimes you need to give people space to kind of get themselves back together.'

The show had been massively successful, and Fox quickly made plans for another season, dubbed *The Simple Life 2: Road Trip*. It was to air in the summer of 2004. This time, the idea was that they would drive around the South in a pink pick-up truck and live in a trailer. They would not be allowed credit cards or mobile phones, and would have to work their way around the country, taking jobs to earn their keep. Some of the tasks they took on were as farm hands, sausage makers, fishers, cattle ranchers, playing mermaids, beauty salon staff and even deputy sheriffs. They stayed at trailer parks and with different families, and once at a nudist resort, where they worked as maids. And it was somewhere warmer: a calculated move on the part of the producers. 'Quite honestly, we went there for the weather,' said one. 'We knew it was going to give Paris and Nicole the opportunity to dress the way they usually like to dress, which is usually with very little clothes.'

The unscripted first season provided a roadmap for the second, giving the creators of the show areas to improve on or skip, as required. 'We do have a pretty good idea going in – because of the families chosen, because of the job situations, knowing the way Paris and Nicole react to things – what we'll probably get,' said executive producer Jon Murray. 'But we don't know for sure, and that's what keeps it edgy and real. Last season, we came up with this idea of the crazy sound effects we use. We sort of punctuate, tell the audience, "Oh, this is funny" or "This is a weird moment." This season, we had an extra camera – always one on the persons Paris and Nicole were dealing with and one on them. So we were able to get reaction shots that helped with the comedy, which made editing easier.'

Once again, the audience's lack of certainty about the stars' ineptitude was key – were they playing up for the cameras, or were they really that clueless? 'The times when they might try to be funny, those are things that may or may not work. We find the best stuff just happens because they're Paris and Nicole. Sometimes it's sort of fun because you're not sure. When Paris puts the metal pot in the microwave, you're going, "Does she really not know you don't do that?"'

The trailer aspect of the show added another dimension: these were girls who were used to their creature comforts. Denying them what they were used to was all part of the entertainment. 'They certainly love doing the publicity,' said Murray. 'They certainly love walking the red carpet. They love all of that. But being on a road trip for 30 days, the novelty for them wore off pretty quickly. They did not enjoy going to bed in that trailer each night. And that's part of what made the show good. And we just had to keep saying, "No, you need to do that." But it's amazing as I look at the tape, there are a lot of times when they're having a great time together, although they both would say, "Oh, I'd never want to do that again."'

The heightened profile meant that the new show wasn't the only thing on the agenda; Nicole was also recording an album, and had been short-listed for a part in the Broadway production of Rent. This kind of thing was, at least, a little more what she had originally had in mind when she had first decided that fame was going to be the career choice for her. 'My plan was not to be a celebrity. My plan was to be a singer and an entertainer. I wanted to go to NYU, major in musical theater, do Broadway, and come out with an album. Unfortunately, I started fucking up when I was in my teens.' *The Simple Life* had surprised her with its success, but maybe it would be a bridge to better things. 'I never thought it would take on a life of its own. And the fame came before the success.'

The train ride continued with the third series, *The Simple Life* 3: Interns. Rather than try to repeat their success and risk things getting stale, Fox programming heads changed the formula again. It began shooting in October 2004, with release scheduled for January 2005 – with minimal editing and only 20 minute episodes, this was fast and cheap TV for the station to produce.

The third season would see them taking public transport – the iconic Greyhound bus – across the country at regular intervals, instead of going back to their nomadic existence in a pink pick-up and trailer parks. With them would travel three miniature dogs and twelve suitcases of clothes and other paraphernalia. Before they left, Paris and Nicole took the opportunity to splash out to the tune of $50,000 at a jewellery store. It was the last time they would be able to spend so freely for a while; in this series, they would be working their way around the country with a variety of jobs again, in a series of internships for different professions. Their first was at an auto shop, where they turn up two hours late on day one and are given a number of tasks that seem to over-tax them. Although the boss seems a little nonplussed when they tell him they're not wearing underwear, which is uncomfortable with the jumpsuits, they at least get to ride around in a police car – without the handcuffs this time.

Once again, the network shaped the material and scripted it so that it's never entirely clear how much viewers were supposed to be laughing with the two, and how much at them. 'So is this blue collar or white collar?' and 'Is Jersey a city or a state?' are two questions that leave the audience wondering whether Paris and Nicole can possibly be as dumb as they seem. On one occasion, working at a funeral home, the girls drop an urn and end up vacuuming up ashes from the floor; a public outcry led to the admission by Fox that this was staged, and that all that was spilt was a mixture of cat litter and cement. Either way, the network knew what they were doing; the whole point of it was that here were two rich, self-absorbed girls who were insensitive to anyone's needs but their own. They were simply giving their viewing public what they wanted. The next week was potentially even worse; the two girls were working as nurses for a plastic surgeon, who was carrying out liposuction and eyebrow lifts. 'Nicole is doing great,' the surgeon said. 'Paris, I don't know if she is cut out for this work.' Fortunately, he stopped short of allowing her to do stitches – even though she argued that she could tie bows in her shoes.

Unfortunately, despite the show's success, this series would be the last for Fox. Ratings for the second series had started at around 10 million, and had climbed afterwards; the third series started with over 13 million, though was down to 4 million by the end. (Part of the reason for the boost was that it was lead-in by American Idol.)

After the third season finished, with the girls being chased by paparazzi and still the best of friends, things soured between them. They had been close for over 20 years; now, however, matters would transpire that would create a very public rift between them that would last for the better part of two years.

The reason for the long-running feud was never publicly admitted, but rumours suggest that it may have involved Paris's infamous sex tape, titled 'One Night in Paris'. Nicole, it was alleged, showed this to the guests at a party. (Another rumour suggested that Paris had told Nicole's parents about her drug problems.) Needless to say, Paris found this utterly humiliating and severed connections with her childhood pal.

Nicole, for her part, strenuously denied that this had been the cause. Her version of events – which didn't entirely ring true – was that the two had just grown apart over time. 'I would never do that I'm sure it stirs up controversy, which I'm sure that Paris loves but I really have nothing bad to say about her. Today, we're no longer friends There's nothing that really happened, we've just grown apart.' Paris didn't agree – though she wouldn't say what the reason for the bust-up was either. 'It's no big secret that Nicole and I are no longer friends,' Paris said in a statement in April 2005. 'Nicole knows what she did, and that's all I'm ever going to say about it.'

As the feud continued, it deepened and became more unpleasant. At one stage, a couple of months after Paris's statement, Nicole appeared to suggest that her former friend was waging a war of harassment against her by means of prank phone calls late at night. 'Nicole has been getting phoney phone calls very late at night, practically every night, and she suspects the culprit is her ex-best friend. Nicole doesn't have proof, but she's almost sure it's Paris,' a friend supposedly told *Femalefirst*.

One of the strangest aspects of the Paris/Nicole fall-out was the popular reaction to it. Some cynical entrepreneurs realised there was an opportunity here. 'I mean, people really banked off of it,' Nicole told AP. 'There were Team Paris and Team Nicole shirts. We didn't make them, you know. And it was really awkward when people would ask me to sign them because I'm not going to sign them. It's true! Like, I'm not going to sign a Team Nicole shirt that says, "Yeah, I'm against Paris" or anything like that, you know.'

The rift between them also called into question the future of their career as America's favourite ditzes. Fox now had a major problem: if the two weren't even on speaking terms, how could they possibly co-operate enough to embarrass themselves on-screen? Paris's solution was to swap Nicole for one of their mutual friends, Kimberly Stewart, daughter of Rod Stewart. This must have been particularly galling for Nicole, since Kimberly had been one of her closest friends since childhood, too. Fox issued a statement denying that they were considering this option. 'We are currently discussing internally the creative direction of the next "*The*

Simple Life." We are huge fans of both Paris Hilton and Nicole Richie and look forward to solidifying our plans for the next installment.'

Paris would later release a song, 'Jealousy', which was to feature in her debut album, Paris, in 2006. Much was made of the lyrics, which were apparently inspired by their fall-out. 'It's a song about any girl. Any girl has a girlfriend that's jealous of you. It's the meanest, most evil thing that can take over you. I brought her on *The Simple Life*, and all of a sudden she became this different person,' *Contactmusic* quoted Paris. 'She dropped her old friends and now she's someone else. That's not the girl I know. That's similar to the lyrics in Jealousy.' Releasing a song about her former friend was a serious act of one-upmanship for Paris.

The Fox execs finally had to admit that another series wasn't going to work under the existing circumstances. Reluctantly, they cancelled plans for the fourth season. 'We did not see a place for "*The Simple Life*" on our schedule this season,' they claimed. All was not lost, however, with other stations hoping to pick up the idea. 'We're disappointed that "*The Simple Life*" will not continue on Fox where it has

performed so well, but we believe this series...
is still a dynamic and valuable franchise. We
hope to be able to announce a new network
partner in the coming days.' The production
company responsible for the show stated,
'We're very excited about the creative plans for
the next group of episodes, and are confident
this situation will be remedied quickly.' Some
were hopeful; Paris, when questioned, didn't
seem to have considered the show's future at all.
'I'm really excited about my movie projects, my
new album and all my various other business
ventures,' she told one magazine.

Meanwhile, Nicole was busy with her own
personal life. Back in 2004 she had started to
date a man called Adam Goldstein, a club DJ.
Goldstein was also known as DJ AM. In February
of 2005, the pair were engaged. Goldstein
seemed like a perfect match for Nicole, sharing
some of her love of fashion, rehab and – one
Nicole would pick up as a direct result of their
later split – a weight problem. (He had even
had gastric bypass surgery.) In fact, the drug
problems had originally been a bar to their
relationship – he wasn't interested in her when
they first met. 'He's seven years sober, and at
the time, you know, I wasn't. And we knew

each other on a very acquaintance hi-hi level. But we never got set up or anything like that. It just kind of happened that we happened to hang out one day. And the first day we hung out, we never stopped hanging out. We've been together ever since.'

Harper's Bazaar commented, 'Nicole is also engaged to her live-in beau, Adam Goldstein, a successful 32-year-old Philadelphia-raised deejay who goes by the name DJ AM and is seven years sober, she says. His hair Dax-waxed into a Mohawk, AM has got a brooding gaze, 500 pairs of Nikes in his closet, and is rarely photographed without a skull T-shirt and dog tags. He, too, had a weight issue and lost nearly 155 pounds over the past two years after gastric-bypass surgery. A cushion-cut pink sapphire brightens Nicole's finger, but she discreetly declines to dangle the precise number of carats.' As it happened, Paris Hilton was also engaged – this time to the Greek shipping heir, Paris Latsis. It was her third engagement. In her case, she featured in the papers perusing rings with 'ice cube-size diamonds'.

In an interview with CosmoGirl, Nicole talked about how her life had changed in the past couple of years, and how she had moved on from her wayward days before *The Simple Life* gave her a reason to behave herself. 'Today I'm not tempted to use drugs or anything like that. Now when problems come my way, I have tools to deal with them. I'm a solver: If there's a problem, I don't whine about it – I try to solve it. I just really like to be logical now – to pick the battles that matter and face them. I learned that you can deal with reality and still have fun. Everything shouldn't be so serious all the time. I like to enjoy life, and I want to continue to always enjoy it.'

Regarding her fiancé, she said, 'Adam and I will probably get married next summer. We met three years ago, through mutual friends, and he's one of the few people, besides my parents and my dogs, who know me better than anyone. I know how lucky we are to have such an incredibly open and honest relationship, and the most important thing in my future is for me to have a big family. I've always said that someday I want five kids – three girls and twin boys. And of course I want dogs and cats! I have a lot to look forward to, you know? And now I'm in such a good place in my life that I'd never want to take a step backward.' (Words that might haunt her two years later.)

The idea of Nicole marrying was of interest to the Fox executives who had lifted her to stardom in *The Simple Life*; they thought that she and AM might draw some viewers if they featured in a new reality TV show about newly-weds. Nicole wasn't convinced. 'I've never, ever thought about that,' she said. 'I hold my relationship really sacred, and he's not an in-front-of-the-camera kind of guy anyway.' Plus, doing a reality show like Simple Life was one thing; letting the cameras see every aspect of her life and marriage was entirely another. 'No one's been in my home or anything like that. It wasn't really my reality.'

Early indications were that the wedding would happen in Santa Barbara in the summer. She intended to have a long engagement; 'Why rush?' she asked. 'I'll be married for the rest of my life. I just really wanted to make sure that I was doing the right thing.' Making sure things went well extended to having elephants present at the ceremony, on the grounds that they were good luck. Unfortunately, her extensive plans didn't wash too well with her fiancé – who, at least one report suggested, was 'disgusted by her flamboyant plans.' 'I want elephant rides and swans. He wants, like five people at our wedding – our close friends and family only,' she complained.

Perhaps this was one of many differences, but the relationship didn't get as far as the next celebrity divorce. The couple broke up on December 7, 2005, although they would sell plenty more celebrity magazines and tabloid column-inches by continuing an on-off relationship over the next few months. The reason, said Nicole, was that 'I've been in really good relationships, and I've been in really bad ones, but the one thing that stands out about Adam is that I can be myself.'

Around the same time that she was breaking up from DJ AM, her face and feet were gaining some attention. In her first endorsement deal, she had been signed up as the new face of Bongo, screening in March. She appeared in the adverts with blond hair, considerably thinner than she had been seen in recent months. 'The last Bongo ads were done by Rachel Bilson, and I thought they were really cute, so I was really excited to do it. I love having my picture taken!' she told WWD. The Bongo team knew how to make her feel at home at the photoshoot, building a doghouse out of denim for her puppies (Foxxy Cleopatra and Honey Child). DJ AM was also invited to play some music. They also served her Taco Bell – her favourite food – on a silver platter.

She had also been signed up as the new ambassador for Jimmy Choo, the shoemaker who shot to fame to rival Manolo Blahnik, and whose creations are worn by the likes of Victoria Beckham and, perhaps most well-known, Sex and the City's Sarah Jessica Parker. Choo president Tamara Mellon chose her for the new campaign, saying, 'Nicole has such an incredibly sophisticated look and fabulous sense of style and I am so proud of this collaboration.' Nicole was pretty happy about the development too. 'I'm so excited to be part of the campaign. I've been a Jimmy Choo fan since I was a little girl, and it's such an honour to represent them, I feel like a princess.'

In March 2006, rumours surfaced that she and DJ AM were back together after they were seen together in LA, and taking a holiday together in Mexico. 'They decided to try again,' a friend supposedly told *People magazine*. 'They never stopped caring about each other. They really are so happy together... It was only a matter of time before they got back together.' However, the engagement ring was nowhere to be seen.

For his 33rd birthday on March 30th, Nicole threw him a surprise party at Pure Nightclub in Las Vegas. 'This is his eighth year of sobriety. I'm so proud of you,' she toasted him in front of their friends. 'You've come so far and I love you so much.' Other sources suggest that AM didn't look too happy at the event. 'He was keeping to himself at the party... but he was working. He could have just been concentrating.'

 ""It wasn't to last. In May, Nicole's publicist, Cindy Guagenti, released a statement on her behalf after rumours began to swirl about a break up. 'We are confirming that we have amicably separated. The rumors and speculations as to why we have separated are both false and hurtful. Current allegations as to why our relationship has changed are completely untrue. We would greatly appreciate our privacy.' No further details were provided.

In the long run, Goldstein's drug problems did get the better of him. In August 2009 he was found dead in his apartment, along with a crack pipe and prescription medication. He had recently survived a plane crash that had killed four other people, and badly injured Travis Barker, Blink 182's drummer. Apparently, the trauma of this may have contributed to a relapse. Paris Hilton, who had known him since she was 15, tweeted: ""R.I.P. AM, I love you and you are already missed so much. My heart and prayers go out to his family and close friends. God bless. :('

Nicole Richie on Malibu Beach,
California, America - 13 Aug 2006

Carrera Sunglasses Escape at Chateau Marmont, Hollywood, Los Angeles, Jul 2010

*The Art of Elysium's 3rd
Annual Black Tie Gala
'Heaven', Beverly Hills,
Los Angeles, Jan 2010*

3.

A NEW LEAF

Alongside her personal ups and downs, Nicole's work was experiencing something of a diversification too. Almost unbelievably, she had written a novel, which was released at the end of 2005. The book was called *The Truth About Diamonds*. It was, in reality, a thinly-veiled account of her own life, adapted for the mass market, and was intended to be the first of two novels along the same lines. The plot follows a twenty-something woman called Chloe Parker, who was adopted at the age of seven by a famous musician and his wife, who engages in a wild socialite life with Hollywood celebs and runs foul of the press and police, ending up in rehab. Despite the self-evident similarities to her own life, Nicole was at pains to state that it was not an autobiography. 'I'm only 23, and besides, I would never dish on celebrities,' she maintained. 'Like, that would be so rude. Everyone would hate me.'

Naturally, the publishers made good use of her image to sell books. Regan Books' own Judith Regan commented, 'I love everything about her. She's like a little beam of light' – adding, 'I really regret that she's not available for my son.' The launch was a media event of huge proportions, with paparazzi out in force and the great and the good present from many different magazines. 'She is somebody that our readers really look up to as a fashion icon in the making,' said *Teen Vogue*'s Nicole Vecchiarelli. The reason why, suggested Carolyn Lluberes of Wilhelmina Models, was because Nicole was a 'survivor'. 'She sends the message that, "Yes, I've fallen, but I can get up with dignity." I never get star-struck, but to see her is really inspiring.'

And, of course, Lionel Richie was there, present at a moment of publicity for his daughter that he could be proud of. 'She's my little girl,' he told one reporter. 'I'm having a pride attack right now. Two years ago she was trying to get her life together, and now she's so clear.'

Her father was taking all of this new media

attention in his stride. 'Nicole is the new superstar of the family, which I'm loving,' he said. 'She's Miss Fashion Icon. She has such a sense of style, such grace. I'm all puffed up with pride and the buttons are popping on my shirt as I speak.' And, he suggested, it was nice that she was spending someone else's money – namely her own. 'And I'm just happy she's buying her own clothes now, thank you. I was just about to go broke.' In 2005 *People magazine* suggested that Paris Hilton got paid $5 million for the third season of the show, and although Nicole wasn't happy about receiving less, she can't have been too far behind.

In truth, though, Lionel recognised that Nicole's fame was a double-edged sword. It wasn't the same type of fame he was used to; this was Celebrity, which was inseparable from its media hype and attendant intrusions. 'I can always tell when Nicole is about to visit,' he grinned. 'There's a helicopter overhead. I look up and think, "Yup, that's Nicole coming." And then there are five cars following her. It's tough, but she's handling it.'

'Being famous is a wonderful thing as long as you're lying by the pool in Miami,' he continued. 'But this is work. To fly to London, to Paris, to New York, to do the shows, and then to stay up late and try to be the party person... it doesn't work. Balance is what she has to learn. I did too. At the end of every album and every tour, I would end up in hospital suffering from exhaustion. She's now learning the same thing.' Asked how he figured out how to keep it together, he said, 'How did I get straight? I got married. You come home and you have dinner. She's single going through all of this; I'm surprised she gets a meal a day. And, of course, she just broke up with her fiancé, which doesn't help...'

Lionel obviously liked DJ AM, and was sad for both of them when they split. But he also recognised the effect of the changing times. 'He's a nice guy, a sweetheart; they love each other very much. But they are at the beginning of their careers. Back when I was growing up, you could break up and nobody knew. Now everybody knows before you do. It's hard. Nicole has had the roughest time. Even I have to question whether I could have gone through some of the stuff she's been through.'

At this point, the first rumblings were beginning

that perhaps the stress was too much for her and that Nicole had traded one problem for another; since *The Simple Life* first aired, she was looking an awful lot thinner – some said, worryingly so. 'I have a very strong group of people around me, and if I had problem, that many wouldn't be quiet about it. We would take care of it,' she stated. 'I've never owned a scale,' she told the *New York Times*, 'but I think people forget that I was on this earth 21 years before "Simple Life" and I've always been very thin. I just went through a heavier stage.' To prove it, she wolfed down a cheeseburger and McNuggets in front of the reporter. 'Spend a day with me and you'll see how anorexic I am. I eat like there's no tomorrow.'

The book reached number 32 on the *New York Times* Best Seller List – hardly stellar, though nothing to be sniffed at, either. Nicole had actually been asked to write books in the past. Publishers had approached her trying to commission advice projects, as well as her actual autobiography (as opposed to the thinly-veiled and hotly-denied roman à clef this one actually was). She chose fiction, she says, because this medium allowed her to alter and improve her own personal story. 'When I spoke to my dad because he's a writer and I really wanted to know what to write about he said, "You have to write about what you know and your experiences," so that's what I did and I just made it a lot more exciting,' she told CNN.

There may have been another, related motive. Paris Hilton had clearly got one up on her by writing a song, 'Jealousy', that obviously referenced themes from their public feud. A novel enabled her to write about Paris in return, amplifying her unattractive characteristics in the cause of making a good story. The book's protagonist stars in a reality show with a friend, Simone Westlake, who turns into an enemy... The description of Miss Westlake goes, 'Simone was leggy and tall, though no one knows exactly how tall because she'd never been seen out of pumps since puberty... not even in her night-vision skin flicks, filmed strictly for private use, of course.' Anyone familiar with Paris Hilton's early filmography, much of which was filmed using night vision, could hardly fail to see the inspiration. 'It's not her,' Nicole nevertheless claimed. 'I've come across many people in my life that are like that.' Of course.

Westlake wasn't the only one of her friends

who bore a suspicious resemblance to people she was close to in reality. Her fiancé on paper was DJ Ray, a man who has needed gastric bypass surgery in the past, like AM. There's even a 'Nicole Richie'. Critics seized on this as evidence for her lack of imagination and literary talent. Nicole claimed she wrote the book herself, rather than have it ghosted by someone else, but there was still the cloud hanging over her that the only reason for her success might be that her father was famous, and her personal life a tabloid staple.

Pushed on the similarities, she admitted, 'Well, Chloe the character is loosely based on myself but no other characters are based on anybody else.' Simone, she said, 'is the person that she gets to campaign with and Simone really represents just all of the people that I have kind of pushed out of my life after I got out of rehab and kind of decided to really become an adult, you know. You just kind of press the delete button on people that are not good for you.' The interviewer pushed on, 'Paris lost this device and stars' numbers were released on the Internet. It was a big deal right? I mean that is exactly what happened in her life and it's in the book.' This was a reference to a recent incident in which Paris's phone account had been hacked by a teenage boy who posted all of her numbers – including dozens of celebrities – on the internet.

Asked if Chloe and Simone got on in the book, Nicole answered, 'They don't. They're just two completely separate people. They're just – they're just really not the same people. They were more friends when Chloe kind of wasn't in her right head space.'

Aside from the writing project and the on/off relationship and wedding plans, Nicole had plenty else to keep her busy. She was working on an album of pop/funk music – new ground for her, but something she had always wanted to do since she was a child, growing up with a famous singer for a father. 'I've been singing my whole life, actually,' she told a CNN interviewer. 'And I play instruments. I play piano, violin and cello. I'm just recording it right now. It is like a mixture of pop and funk, I guess.' Asked about the content of the songs – no doubt with her own autobiographical novel and Paris's 'Jealousy' dig in mind – she answered, 'The songs are about what I know. Again, about just growing up and becoming a woman. The book is more based on growing up in Hollywood and stuff like that. I mean, my album is more based on just being a girl no matter who you are. Facing everyday problems being a woman.'

Her influences in this project were numerous and diverse, and she cites Gwen Stefani, Britney Spears, Cat Stevens, Prince and Metallica among them – Britney being a particular favourite. 'I think just she's a great all-around performer.' As it happened, her arch-enemy Paris Hilton also happened to be bringing out an album around the same time. Nicole took this in her stride, hinting that Paris was musically untalented and untrained, and that there would be no competition from her. 'I have a musical background, grown up around musicians. I've always known that this is what I was going to do. So her putting out an album to me is the same thing as anybody putting out an album.' However, she acknowledged that breaking into the business was difficult and, Paris aside, there was plenty of other competition. 'I think that it's definitely difficult. I mean, you know, there are a lot of artists that I think are really great that didn't make it. So, I don't really know, to be honest, what it takes to make it. I think it just really depends.'

Whereas for her book, the critics suggested that her success was down to her father's name, in this case it would be the opposite. Having a father who was a successful and talented singer would only raise the bar for her – she was entering a field where she would be judged more harshly than most others. And, Nicole said, it was highly intimidating for her to have him around while she was working on it. Lionel must have found it hard, too – having so much to say that could be useful to her, but trying to stay at arm's length so as not to interfere.

There was always the danger that he would get too close and overstep the mark with her. 'He really actually tries not to because he knows that that is the best thing. So he's actually been really good about it. But I actually went into the studio a few months ago and it was the same studio that I grew up in, that he recorded in the '80s! It was a lot smaller, actually, than I remembered. But it was really cool just to see, just to be able to record in a studio that I grew up in.'

In fact, she was so intimidated by her father's talent that she didn't even offer to let him listen to any of her songs. 'He can listen to it, just not when I'm there,' she conceded, professing shyness and embarrassment whenever anyone even watched *The Simple Life* when she was present.

Perhaps the book was a surprising career move for Nicole, and the nascent music career aspirational if not out of the blue. Something that did not come as a surprise at all was her growing influence in fashion. After all, by now she had spent three seasons tripping round the different settings of *The Simple Life* in her high heels and designer clothes, next to Paris Hilton. No doubt some of Paris's demeanour (she used to be a model) had rubbed off on Nicole – who, one writer in Harper's Bazaar pointed out, 'even poses like Paris, all pouty and runway-ready'.

Her transformation from style consumer to fashion trend setter had started in May 2004, when she appeared on Oprah with her father – discussing, amongst other things, her troubled childhood and drug addiction. To help give her confidence and prepare her for the publicity, Lionel had hired a stylist called Rachel Zoe Rosenzweig – a woman famous in Los Angeles for having worked with the likes of Jessica Simpson and Lindsay Lohan. Zoe, as she is known, made some suggestions, and Nicole would visit some of the classiest shops in LA to make good on them. 'A lot of people think I shop every single day because they see pictures of me shopping, but that's the only place the paparazzi are going to get me,' she told Harper's Bazaar. 'I'm really not into the whole diva thing. I don't walk around L.A. with a bodyguard.'

Zoe continued to be a profound influence on Nicole, and this was a decidedly double-edged sword. The fashionista – who allegedly charges around $6,000 a day for her services – is one of the most powerful women in style, but she courts controversy with that. An analysis from the Telegraph explains why. 'Her most devoted clients, such as Nicole Richie, Keira Knightley and wild child actress Lindsay Lohan, are decidedly scrawny and all battle speculation about their weight. Known as the Zoe-bots, they have matching toothpick arms and sunken faces barely able to support the fashionably enormous sunglasses their svengali encourages them to wear. To her detractors Zoe – who weighs no more than a kitten herself – has therefore replaced Kate Moss as the number one culprit for society's collective eating disorder. Some say she is the architect of size 0 mania – a fad for super skinniness that is spreading from Zoe's home town of LA around the world.' Size zero would become considerably less cool after a model died of fasting-induced heart failure in Madrid, in 2006, but it already had plenty of critics.

Zoe recounts her first meeting with Nicole, who had already featured on *The Simple Life*, next to the thinner and then far more fashionable Paris. At the time, Nicole was considerably heavier than she is now. 'Nicole showed up to meet me in an airport wearing a sweat suit, with a leopard-print neck pillow tied around her neck and an "I Love LA" cap and her hair in pig tails. I think she was doing it to torture me.'

And so the weight began to come off Nicole, as the stylish, expensive clothes went on. Stella McCartney, Chloe and Chanel were particular favourites. Plus, instead of the bright colours she used to wear, she moved towards more understated browns and black: 'I don't like to draw that kind of attention to myself. You'll never see me in fluorescents.' Despite Zoe's input, Nicole did most of the actual shopping herself. Her hair also changed dramatically, from dreadlocks (using hair extensions) to a soft, shoulder-length cut. She had had this done for a part as a cheerleader in the teen film Kids in America, her film début, released in 2005 but filmed in mid-2004, just after her Oprah makeover. 'And I liked it so much, I kept it.'

In 2005, a couple of years into *The Simple Life* – two seasons of which had seen her change almost beyond recognition – she waved away comment about her makeover. 'A girl can change her style, can't she?' the Chicago Sun-Times quoted her. It was, she claimed, just about 'growing up'.

Moreover, she argued, she is naturally skinny but when she started on *The Simple Life*, she was much heavier than usual, thanks to rehab. Regular sessions with her trainer, Adam Irnster, helped fix that. 'I do cardio and boring stuff. But I prefer the fun stuff, like the rowing machine and this surfing machine Adam got for me,' she said.

Alongside the press for her creative projects, she was also garnering some less welcome media interest along the way. It was nothing like Paris's tape, but it still excited the tabloids and magazines in a way that quickly grew tiresome – and would be just as persistent. From losing the extra weight in 2004 and 2005, Nicole's weight had suddenly plummeted at the beginning of 2006, not long after she broke up with DJ AM for the first time. Alongside the unhappiness of this event, her stylist Rachel Zoe was allocated some of the blame.

Nicole wasn't the only one of the Zoe-bots (pronounced to rhyme with 'robots' – as Zoe's name is pronounced to rhyme with 'go') to radically slim down. Jessica Simpson and Mischa Barton of the OC caught the paparazzi's attention when they appeared, skeletally thin, in their bikinis. Nicole – who Zoe called 'my little Barbie doll' for her now exquisite style – was melting away. She started to wear a red bracelet; she claimed this was a religious symbol. Followers of Kabbalah – a strand of Jewish mysticism recently made famous by Madonna and other celebs – often wear the red wool on their left hand. On the right – as worn by Nicole – it is frequently a symbol of anorexic pride, the so-called 'friends of Ana'. That is how many people interpreted it, at any rate, and not without cause. The Telegraph pointed out how, whatever the reason for the red bracelet, what it did do was draw attention to her wrists, which were now exceptionally thin: 'The smallest on any human being over the age of 12,' Zoe had commented.

It wasn't looking good for Nicole, and Zoe was getting some of the fallout for the wider size-zero trend and its physically and psychologically unhealthy implications. 'That girl Rachel Zoe definitely has something to do with it,' one article accused. 'I've seen her eat – and she doesn't. It's the classic "living for clothes, dying for fashion".' Another observed, 'I've worked with Rachel all day on a shoot, and basically, she drank a giant latte and smoked a bunch of cigarettes.'

Zoe herself naturally went on the defensive. 'I don't think it's fair to say that I'm responsible because I'm a thin person, that because I'm influencing their style I'm influencing what they eat. There was this crazy rumour that I was getting diet pills from Mexico and distributing them. I was like, "Okay, I've never even tried cocaine. I don't do drugs – I'm too much of a control freak."'

'There's a small grey area between being too skinny and being a thin person,' Zoe commented. 'An eating disorder is a very sad thing – it kills people. I would never in a million years tell a client they had to lose weight. There's a size for everybody. People don't realise that I've worked with people who are size 8 and 10.'

The fact remained, however, that Zoe and people like her were extremely influential in the field. 'Stylists are now critical to the fashion market and Rachel is incredibly important in the industry,' said *Teen Vogue* editor Amy Astley. 'She has kick-started many of the trends you see today. She, and others like her, have opened up the fashion industry so it's not just for insiders. Now everyone knows about labels because they read about their celebrities wearing them.' This also encompassed celebrities like Nicole, who was rapidly becoming a source of fashion advice and inspiration.

The end of 2005 had seen Fox drop *The Simple Life* from their schedule; word was that they couldn't see how to make it work with the two girls at war with each other. Fortunately for Nicole, though, the cable network E! did believe it still had potential, and negotiated terms for a fourth season. This one would be called 'Til Death Do Us Part, and would see the girls travel around their home county of California, playing housewife and mother in a series of families. There was still the seemingly insurmountable problem of how to deal with the fact that they hated each other. E! cleverly circumvented this issue by simple virtue of not having them share screen time. As one review wrote, 'Paris Hilton and Nicole Richie are still acting their parts of simpleton celebrities thrust into the "real" lives of regular folk, but during the contractually obligated production of what had become an astonishingly popular show, the poor little rich girls were in the midst of a bitter feud. They hated each others' guts, weren't speaking, and thanks to the machinations of their individual publicity experts, the whole world knew it. Consequently, the two rarely share screen time together except for ample sequences of split-screening, which makes for an even more bizarre pairing for two dim-witted million-heiresses who remain famous for nothing more that, well, being famous. Season four consists of a variety of slices of suburban Los Angeles family life with the wife/mother role being taken over on alternate days by either Paris or Nicole. As usual, they sneer and make fun of the lower class that they visit – all the while showing absolutely no class of their own.'

In fact, continued the review, the feud actually helped in some ways – after all, reality TV has never been about contriving happy endings. Conflict is its life blood. 'But as with the prior seasons, the can't-look-away-from-the-train-wreck aspect is the thing that keeps our attention. They hate us and we hate them, so it's the very definition of symbiotic entertainment. Since they also hate each other there's an extra element of amusement; only don't think too hard lest the fine line between amusement and contempt disappears. Who knows if their feud was real or made up by the genius publicity machines behind their fame...'

Car-crash TV, too, was the growing revelation evident in season 4 that Nicole was struggling with some serious health issues. 'One thing that's not made up and definitely not comical is the gruesome change in Nicole Richie's body as her issues with low body weight reveal itself over the course of the episodes.'

Nicole, for her part, enjoyed working on *The Simple Life* 4, even if her friendship with Paris was over – the rest of it was fun. 'You know what, I really have fun filming no matter what. I love doing the show. It's a lot of fun. I love the producers and the directors and, you know, it's a really fun show,' she enthused.

Not all of the families she was placed with shared her love of the concept. On one occasion that made the news, she asked an eleven-year-old boy if he thought she was attractive. Well, actually, what she really asked him was whether he thought she was a 'Milf'. Understandably, the boy didn't know what she meant, and told her this. 'It means a "Mother I'd like to f***,"' she told him. The boy's father overheard her teaching him new acronyms, and was naturally livid. He forbid the impromptu footage of the incident be used, refusing to sign consent forms. When it was used anyway, he filed a complaint to the production company. His mother later said that the exchange resulted in an awkward conversation with her son. 'I'm 90 percent mad but a little part of me says, "Stop being a prude." I guess I just don't want my son to grow up that fast,' she said. It was all the more confusing for the fact that Nicole wasn't a mother, and therefore couldn't be a Milf...

If that father was angry, she says another was pleasantly surprised. In one episode, she had to help an expectant father at a Lamaze (antenatal) class. Since his wife was almost due, she couldn't be present, so Nicole stepped in to help. It happened that one of the topics on the agenda was sexual positions. 'I went to a Lamaze class with one of the husbands because the wife was nine months pregnant, so I had to be nine months pregnant. That day they happened to be teaching us about being able to still have sex and they wanted someone to demonstrate, so obviously I did it,' *Contactmusic* quoted her. 'I just demonstrated being in different positions with the husband and straddling him; he loved every second of it.'

The fourth season was aired in June 2006, and gained just 1.3 million viewers – a tenth of its Fox peak. However, for E! this was a fantastic result, tripling or quadrupling its regular viewing figures for the slot. Unfortunately, this also had the effect of pushing Nicole – this time with a worryingly skinny frame – back into the spotlight. Speculation about her weight issues redoubled.

As time went on, so did the weight loss, and

the more weight came off, the more the media flocked around her, eagerly speculating about the causes. In fact, some like the Mail commented that her eating issues had first made her famous as a style guru – along with Zoe's help – and then kept her famous with the additional speculation when it became really unhealthy.

'Her signature "look" – the one which has led *Teen Vogue* to hail her as a "style icon" – is of an undernourished child wearing huge sunglasses. Her thinness has become over the past few years what defines her as a celebrity, and to the shame of the showbusiness media, it is perhaps what keeps her as one, too... the more famous she has become, the thinner she has got – and the more she's been written about. U.S. celebrity magazines, which feature her on their covers almost weekly, have coined a new phrase for Richie – "Scary Skinny" – and, without wishing to be unkind, she has absolutely lived up to that label.'

At a time when size zero (the British equivalent of a size 4 – the average in the UK is a 14) was all the rage and anorexia fashionable in certain subcultures, Nicole was fast becoming a poster-girl for the cause. She was down to 85 pounds – barely more than six stone – and yet still managed to claim that clothes designed for size zeros didn't go far enough. 'My favourite designers don't make stuff that is good for my frame,' she once said. If that wasn't proof of a distorted body image, what was? Then there was her repeated denial of her problem, in the face of overwhelming evidence to the contrary. 'I live a very honest and healthy life,' the Mail quoted her. 'It's not something I think about. It's never been an issue for me, but it's sad when people feel that pressure.'

After some months of this performance, the truth evidently began to dawn on her, and she realised that she was going to have to do something about it. In an interview with Vanity Fair in June 2006 she admitted, 'I know I'm too thin right now, so I wouldn't want any young girl looking at me and saying, "That's what I want to look like." I do know that they will, which is another reason I really do need to do something about it. I'm not happy with the way I look right now.' That, at least, could be considered progress. In the past, she had produced a fine line in denial: at interviews, she would typically sit there at a fast food restaurant, hoovering down junk food, all the while claiming that she wasn't anorexic. And yet the weight stayed off, and the press started to get suspicious that it was all an act for their benefit.

Finally, that autumn, she checked into a medical facility. It wasn't rehab, her publicist was keen to point out, saying that the purpose of the visit was 'to undergo diagnostic treatment to determine why she's not been putting on any weight.' A statement was released: 'She is working with a team of doctors and specialists whose focus is nutrition. It is important to Nicole that she achieve this goal in a healthy way, but this is not a treatment for an eating disorder.' After her comments in Harper's Bazaar, and her admission earlier that year that her on/off relationship with DJ AM had affected her appetite and caused her weight problems, the press didn't find this convincing. News of weekly weigh-ins didn't help her case. (Neither did Paris Hilton, who evidently found it all very amusing – she sent her a biscuit in the fourth series of *The Simple Life*.)

Lionel recognised the danger and – as with the drug arrest – came straight to her defence.

'Everybody says, "Oh, it's anorexia." No, it's not, I promise you. She's been tested and tested and tested. Right now she's desperately trying to get control of her life.'

In 2007, after the worst of the anorexia stories had blown over, she rewrote history again in another Harper's Bazaar interview. 'I eat everything. I always have, contrary to what people think.' The main reason for her weight loss, she said, was simply stress. 'It happens to a lot of people, and I don't understand why people don't understand that it happens to me. I'm not going to lie and say I wasn't really thin at one point, because I was. But it had nothing to do with not eating.' The press, she claimed, hadn't helped, as the speculation only added to the stress that had caused the problem in the first place. 'I'm not saying that I have more problems than everyone else, but people's weight fluctuates, and five or ten pounds is a lot on me.' A diagnosis of hypoglycaemia also gave her a peg to hang the problem on. 'Even though it's not good news, it's good news to me because I didn't know why I was having so many problems.' More recently still, in 2010, she reiterated this denial. 'I felt it was a little unfair to say someone has an eating disorder when they don't. It's extremely insulting and irresponsible. An eating disorder is serious and it's a disease,' she was quoted in the New York Daily News. The pictures of her, she said, did not bear close resemblance to the reality. 'I think when you see me in person, you see that I'm, like, five foot one. I'm a small person. When I was heavier, everyone said I was too heavy. You can't win in the public eye and I find it really hard.'

Meanwhile, there were canny figures behind the scenes who realised that Nicole's weight issues weren't just good news for the gossip mags; they could be good news for her career, too. Benny Medina, producer, manager and record exec to stars including Jennifer Lopez and Mariah Carey, was hired to help kick start her music career. In his own interview with Vanity Fair, he noted how compelling her story was – and how it could be used to their advantage. 'A celebutante in a fight with another celebutante, who socialises with the best of the best, who comes out of a drug addiction into an eating disorder – that's a lot of good copy. Now what do you want to do with it?' The more cynical, or perhaps incisive critics suggested that Medina had been the one who stage-managed Nicole's 'coming out' to the same magazine about her problems – it was all part of the same publicity process.

However much the publicity would help her career, she did realise that it was a double-edged sword; she knew that thousands of teenagers followed her every move and emulated her in every way they could – speech patterns, style and, of course, weight. 'I do recognise that I have a problem and I want to be responsible and fix it and I am on that path now,' she clarified, for their benefit. Doctors, meanwhile, suggested that her weight was 'in the realm of anorexia,' though falling short of making it a medical diagnosis. One psychologist – the vice chair at the psychology department of the Cedars Sinai Medical Centre, the facility in which she was hospitalised in LA, commented: 'We are all concerned and she is concerned, but it's either going to improve or it won't. If it is not anorexia, she should be able to gain the weight. If it ends up being anorexia we will help her with that. I think she is willing to look this one in the eye.'

Unfortunately, for every medical expert concerned with Nicole's health, there were thousands of other people concerned with keeping her dangerously thin. Medina had put his finger on something: this look sold, even if it could be lethal. He practically endorsed her skeletal look in one interview: 'I think she is motivated to be scarily little. The more cheruby Nicole Richie was cute, but she was not the dynamo that this persona is. When she walks into a room now and she's got on the right gear, she looks drop-dead.' He knew that his opinion was shared by many others who looked up to her as an icon. But, he was at pains to state, his interest was not personal: it was purely professional. 'She might be more attractive to me personally if she put on a few pounds, but is that more attractive to the camera, to the clothes she wears and the pages she fills? No. There is an aspirational look. The younger generation has become obsessed with thinness that pushes it to a point of concern.'

On the personal front, things were looking up for Nicole. In September 2006, Nicole started a new but short-lived relationship, this time with a childhood friend, Brody Jenner. Jenner was a reality TV star and socialite, and the son of Olympic decathlete Bruce Jenner. Since the two families had known each other for years, each were pleased at their children's choice. 'I was there when he was born,' said Lionel. 'They grew up together. To see them together now is like, "Where are you going with this?" But they're having a wonderful time. He's a great kid.' Jenner's mother also claimed to be happy for them. 'Nicole is like my godchild. She's a darling girl, very intelligent and very together. I think they're very cute. Will they get married? Who knows? He's young and so is she,' *Contactmusic* quoted them.

The answer to her question became clear fairly soon; within a month or two they had split. A message appeared on her MySpace page: 'I know there are rumors regarding my "breakup" with Brody Jenner. The truth is, we were never really together. We hung out, and he's a nice guy, but my heart was never in it. Anything further is just a cry for publicity.' Ouch. Nicole had started seeing a new boyfriend, Joel Madden, the lead singer for the pop punk band Good Charlotte. Madden had broken up with his long-term girlfriend, Lizzie McGuire actress Hilary Duff, in November 2006, and before the end of the year was dating Nicole. The relationship became serious very quickly – which wasn't to everyone's liking. Benji

Madden, Joel's twin brother and bandmate, was reported to have been concerned at how fast things were going; Duff, needless to say, wasn't impressed either.

'I love him, he's a really great person,' she told *Contactmusic*. 'But I broke up with Joel, and when I decided that breaking up was the right decision.' The one-month gap between her and Nicole – if that – was a slap in the face. 'I had to think through all the things I was going to have to deal with. One of them was seeing him with someone else. It's definitely difficult to see him move on so quickly,'

But Nicole thought the world of him. For someone who has lived her life in the spotlight, she is actually quite careful about what she says about her romantic relationships, preferring to keep at least this one personal area out of the magazines to the extent that it is possible. 'I like really pale, I like really skinny, I like people that kind of look homeless,' she once said of Madden. 'Back in the day, it would have been David Bowie, Jimi Hendrix...'

She had also patched up her friendship with Paris Hilton. And that, in turn, made a new series of *The Simple Life* considerably easier to film.

Nicole admits that Paris sent her an email, extending the olive branch first. It was Nicole's 25th birthday in September 2006, and they met at the Beverly Hills Hotel and then went back to Lionel Richie's house. The paparazzi were thrilled at this unexpected windfall, and gave chase in their droves. 'I had to have my security men block off the street because it was so crazy. It's really embarrassing for me to say that. It's so silly, ridiculous.' Paris added, 'There were so many, like 20 of them, chasing us. Because they hadn't seen us together in so long, they were freaking out.'

This was actually fairly normal for them; in their downtime, the girls like nothing more than to go to each other's houses and watch Lost – a series to which they are addicted – and eat pasta or toasted cheese sandwiches. 'We are both, believe it or not, homebodies,' Nicole protested to one magazine. 'I'm telling you! I'm not lying! I'll go to her house; she'll go to mine.' It wasn't all clubs and parties.

In October of 2006, the two childhood friends

were spotted eating together at Dan Tana's Steakhouse – a well-known celebrity haunt in Hollywood. Although the steak-house meeting was proof of their renewed friendship, it was not proof of Nicole's recovery from her eating problems. E! had scheduled the production of the fifth series of *The Simple Life* for November 2006, but this had to be postponed while Nicole was in rehab to sort out her weight. In the end, they could not start shooting until March 2007 – the date it was initially scheduled to air. (By March 2007, there were bigger problems for the show's future than Nicole's weight – both girls had attracted a DUI charge and were facing time in jail as a result.)

Nicole is now dismissive of the whole feud. 'I don't know,' she claimed, when asked what it was all about. 'But I can't get mad at her for talking shit about me. We were in a fight!' She reminisced how she and Paris would raise hell even as toddlers. 'When we were little, our parents always wanted to separate us. And I remember, word for word, them saying it's not that it's me and not that it's her. It was the two of us together!'

The Simple Life's producer was heartily relieved

– producing a series with the two on speaking terms was far easier than what they had had to come up with for the fourth series. 'The thing the viewers love is the two girls together,' Jon Murray told the AP. 'America, Paris and Nicole are going to camp.'

The two would be working as camp counsellors at Camp Shawnee, where they would be looking after various different groups. Scary though that was, it was a much better prospect that Murray's original plan, which would be to film them separately again, this time on a desert island 'with a bunch of survivalists'. Given how much they complained when they had their cell phones taken away, they were hardly going to be jumping at the idea of knitting their own toilet paper. Murray, tongue-in-cheek, credits his concept with bringing them back together. 'They reached out to each other in universal disdain for the island concept, and rekindled their friendship.' On a slightly more serious note, he revealed that the fifth series would explore 'what led to the breakdown in the friendship and maybe some of the misunderstandings and things that got in the way.'

Before shooting began, however, the film crew

had to wait for other events to play themselves out. Nicole had entered rehab for her weight issues, but she seemed to be trading one problem for another. In December 2006, drivers in Burbank, LA found themselves dodging a car that was driving the wrong way down the freeway. The police received a number of calls from concerned motorists, just after midnight on December 11. (When they got to the scene, they found Nicole's Mercedes-Benz SUV innocently parked the right way round in the car pool lane.) AP reported: 'Richie, 25, star of *"The Simple Life"* reality series and daughter of pop singer Lionel Richie, was arrested without incident at 1:45 a.m. (PST) after she failed a field sobriety test given by California Highway Patrol officers, CHP Officer Todd Workman said.'

The police moved her to the passenger seat and drove the car off the road. Nicole admitted of her own accord that she had smoked marijuana, and taken the prescription opiate Vicodin. Unlike the last time, no drugs were found in her car. She was given a drug test, booked and released. Bail was $15,000, and her hearing was set for February 7, 2007, two months later. This was embarrassing for Nicole, to say the least – at several points in the past she had suggested that she had been totally clean since her first spell in rehab back in 2003, when she had been found with heroin in her car. That episode had preceded the first series of *The Simple Life*, and this one threatened to derail the last. However, she was in good company. In September, her co-star Paris Hilton had been arrested for drink driving. Her own hearing was set for December 20th – just nine days after Nicole's arrest.

Once again, the great and the good jumped to Nicole's defence. Quincy Jones, producer, musician and composer, long-time friend of Lionel Richie and Nicole's godfather, gave his opinion on the matter to *People magazine*. As someone who had known Nicole virtually all her life, he was qualified to. 'I adore Nicole,' he said. 'I've known her since she was a baby. She's a very smart girl. When she was younger she worked eight hours a day for eight years to become an Olympic figure skater. She's a very talented girl.'

His diagnosis: 'You get caught up in the peer pressure and the hoopla – it's a media frenzy. It's insane. Success doesn't help,' he began.

'Processing success is a major, major, major process.' Jones has seven children, including six daughters, so he knew the territory of raising girls in the fish bowl of Hollywood. 'I try to tell the young kids there are two cardinal rules: You should approach creativity with humility and have your success with grace. It's a gift from God. You don't deserve it. You are a vehicle of a higher power. Don't abuse it.'

Two months later, the case went to court. Paris Hilton's case had run its course by then, and she was on to the next offence. She had pleaded guilty, and in January 2007 received a fine of $1,500 and three years probation. On January 15th, she was caught driving with a suspended licence, and then a few weeks later, she was stopped for doing 70 mph in a 35 zone, again with a suspended licence. Between those new offences and her failure to enrol in the court-ordered alcohol education programme, she wound up with a jail sentence of 45 days. She initially tried to contest the sentence, including collecting an online petition with thousands of signatures, but California governor Arnold Schwarzenegger wasn't interested in letting her off, and the petition sparked an equally popular one from those who wondered why she thought she was above the law. In the end, she dropped the campaign, and resigned herself to her jail time, set for June 5th – after the last series of *The Simple Life* had finished filming.

Nicole's own problems with the law were a little less high profile, but went along the same lines. The initial hearing occurred in February, but fortunately for her the legal process didn't delay shooting of *The Simple Life* more than her admission to hospital for weight issues, a couple of months earlier, had already done.

The fifth series began filming in March, and saw the two girls cluelessly taking on positions of responsibility and pastoral care as camp counsellors. Camp Shawnee would see five different groups with their own unique needs that season: there was Wellness Camp, Pageant Camp, Couples Camp, Survival Camp and Drama Camp. Two episodes of the series were spent on each. Once again, they didn't have any idea what they were doing, and hadn't bothered to take any time to familiarise themselves with what would be required of them and the sorts of things they would need to get along in the camp setting. 'We actually didn't prepare, which I guess was a problem, because we were wearing heels and just not camp-appropriate things,' Nicole told AP. 'But during the fitness camp we wore sweats a lot, which was a nice break.'

Neither of them knew what to expect, as they had never attended camp as children. 'We had fun with everyone who came in. All the camps were completely different. We would have to do all the challenges that they would have to do,' Paris explained. 'We had to stay with them in the same rooms, so, basically, we were living the camp life. It was hard, you know, not having a cellphone service, being away from our friends and our family, but we had each other, so that was a lot of fun.'

'It was interesting,' agreed Nicole. 'It's definitely not for me. I'm not a camper. But I'm glad I did it once. I'm always up to try anything.' Paris, too, was used to different standards. 'I think just being the camp counsellors is a lot different from actually having to go to camp as a kid. But I don't know. I didn't really like the camp life either. I'd rather go to Europe for the summer.'

Obviously, their renewed friendship was also prime material for the interviewers, and the new series raised questions about how they had put the past behind them. 'We've been best friends since we were two years old,' said Paris. 'I don't have any friend I've had as long as Nicole. She's my sister. Everyone has a fight, you know, it's just not going to be publicised and have things construed and changed around. You know, we're friends. We know the truth.

'The media made up a lot of silly stories and you just have to not pay attention to it.' This would be a recurring theme in both of their explanations of the year-long feud: the press blew things out of proportion and reported things that weren't true. Really, they claimed, it was all a big exaggeration. 'Even though it's public, it's not my choice for it to be public, you know,' added Nicole. 'We just had a falling out and it happened to be public. It wasn't my choice at all. And the fact that we're friends again, the fact that that's public isn't my choice at all. I mean, we're human beings and we get into fights, it happens. Well, we had one fight in 23 years, I guess that's a good thing.'

Season 4 had been great for E!, pulling in a million viewers every episode. Season 5, though, saw a decline in the ratings, and halfway through the series they had dropped to 700,000. Later in the year, E! announced that they wouldn't be renewing the series – despite the fact that the girls had contracts for a sixth and seventh if required. It would be the end of a long and prosperous ride for both of them: four years had passed since they started, and for Nicole especially, it had been the making of her. 'I think that originally people thought, "Oh, this is going to be about two spoiled blonde girls who don't know how to do anything, but make fun of people," and that's not what it's about. If anything, we're making fun of ourselves,' Nicole explained about the reason the show had been successful.

'We're very different. We're very opposite, so it's a good balance, you know, between the two... She has strengths where I have weaknesses and I have strengths where she has weaknesses and it really creates a good dynamic.' There were opportunities, of course, especially since one group was Fat Camp. 'I know people are going to say, "Paris and Nicole are thin, and they're going to make fun of fat people,"' Nicole said. 'But that is so not the case at all.' In fact, she would get a harder time about her own weight, since the fifth series was another showcase for her wire-thin body.

'It's about two best friends who are together and I think people can relate to that, because everyone has a best friend,' added Paris. 'We have our secret languages and our secret looks to each other and we just have fun together. It's hard to find a group who can be like that together. I've been doing the show now for five seasons, so I've definitely, you know, learned a lot. I've travelled the world and met different families and different people and, I don't know, just learning about other people. With Nicole, I've been best friends with her my whole life, so I already knew everything about her. I don't know, just that we can survive any situation and we can have fun no matter where we are, as long as we're together.'

Nicole, too, was at pains to point out how well they now got on. 'It's funny because a lot of people, as close as they are, when you spend so much time with someone, it's like you see habits that you know, you're just like, "Ugh, I can't spend this much time with someone." But I love spending time with her and we have so much fun and, you know, I really just look at it as nothing but fun.'

The Richie-Madden Children's Foundation and Sony Cierge UNICEF Tap Project Fundraiser, Los Angeles, Mar 2009

4.

LIFE GETS
LESS SIMPLE

After the last series wrapped, Nicole had some matters she needed to attend to. There was her weight problem, and the court-ordered rehab time; then there was the sentencing itself. All of this would play out over the next few months.

On 19th May she was seen checking into the Beau Monde Treatment Center in Corona Del Mar, California – supposedly for anorexia and her addiction to prescription medication (such as the Vicodin that had helped land her a DUI charge). She weighed just 83 pounds. Alcohol rehab would wait until later.

The first few days were a detox, and then she was able to continue the programme as an out-patient. One 'source' supposedly said, 'Nicole's been a mess for months. Her weight has plummeted.' She wasn't allowed to go cold turkey, as one paper reported; medical staff were concerned about the levels of addiction, and stopping suddenly can be dangerous. 'They didn't want me to quit cold turkey – I could've had a seizure, so they gave me medication,' she said.

In late July – amid early rumours she was pregnant by Madden – Nicole got the news she was fearing: the judge sentenced her to four days in prison. This was hardly serious jail time, but she seemed to realise that she needed the term to shock her out of her bad habits. Unlike Paris Hilton, who tried to have her sentence cancelled with an online petition, Nicole at least had the decency to hold up her hands and accept hers. 'I could have killed someone... I think this was a blessing in disguise,' she said. 'This year has been full of lessons learned and soul searching and realizing I'm an adult. It's time to take responsibility and not take the easy way out. I never want to make a mistake like that again. I never want to possibly take another life in my hands... My life is clearly going to slow down.'

A police official commented to AP on a little of what she could expect. 'She's not gonna be coming in here wearing a miniskirt and pumps. We pretty much go the bare minimum.' House arrest, she had been told, was not an option.

In truth, she had been lucky. It was her second DUI conviction and, pregnant or not, a four-day sentence (96 hours, minus the six she had already spent in detention) was nothing compared to the year she might had got if she hadn't pleaded guilty and made a deal with prosecutors. Plus, she could choose whichever local LA County jail she wanted that would take her. The judge made it clear that she would do the rest of the year if she fell foul of the law again.

The terms of her conviction were that she had to finish her time in jail by 28th September that year, and would need to come back to court in February 2008 to prove that she had kept the other conditions of the sentence. Another state department would decide whether to suspend her licence. She left the court with Madden, surrounded by bodyguards – a nicety she would not be allowed in jail. Speculation was that – if she went to the Burbank jail –

she would be confined to a four by ten foot cell, since the prison had limited facilities for female criminals, and because she was very well known.

In the end, she wound up in the Lynwood facility – where Paris Hilton had done 23 days out of her 45 day sentence, despite her best efforts to convince Schwarzenegger that she shouldn't. Nicole got off more lightly than that – she served just 82 minutes. In fact, she didn't even reach her cell. She made it through fingerprinting, but then guidelines came into play that recommended that, to prevent overcrowding, non-violent offenders who had been sentenced to less than 30 days should usually be released within 12 hours.

For Nicole, this time seems to have been one of genuine soul-searching. Asked whether she thought she was above the law by one magazine, she answered, 'Well, clearly I'm not! Otherwise, it would be smooth sailing. I get caught for everything! Every mistake I make, there's consequences. I don't take anything lightly.' Paris, though, offered a different explanation. 'I think I get in more trouble just because of who I am. The cops do it all the time.

They'll just pull me over to hit on me. It's really annoying. They're like, "What's your phone number? Want to go to dinner?" They won't even give me a ticket. They just pull me over, and the paparazzi, of course, take a picture. All the time. I have so many cops' business cards...'

One good piece of news was made public fairly soon after that: Nicole was confirmed pregnant. And, whilst that was good news in itself, it also meant that she was allowed to drop out of the alcohol rehab ordered by the court. As well as the 18 month course, she was recommended to attend Alcoholics Anonymous meetings – though there was little chance of remaining anonymous under the circumstances.

Jail and rehab all over, it was time to reassess her life – especially in the light of her pregnancy. And it's fair to say that things were looking up. She had Madden, and she had Paris back. And she was coming to terms with the fact that, although everyone took an interest in her, not everyone did so for the right reasons. The press was one obvious example, having built up her fight with Paris and then capitalised on it when they became friends again. 'Our fight was so built up by the press. Half of it wasn't even real,' she told Harper's Bazaar. The press intrusion and manipulation extended to her friends and other's connected to her life. Singer and actress Mandy Moore, for one – someone who otherwise manages to stay above this kind of thing – had started dating her ex, DJ AM, and was quoted in one magazine: 'I'm not Nicole Richie. I'm not like a toothpick, and I never will be.'

Hurtful though this might have been, Nicole had started to realise what was going on. 'Mandy's a really sweet girl. It was a coincidence that she started dating Adam, and the press just went wild with it. She apologized, and I know that she didn't mean anything by it. She's so not malicious.'

More broadly, she had recognised that Hollywood is not good for celebrity friendships; there is so much gossip and back-stabbing that it can be hard to know who your friends are. 'This year, my biggest struggle has been realizing that some people close to me are not good for my life,' she commented. 'I'm a girl and I love to gossip, but when I hear that people I consider friends are talking about me, it really hurts my feelings. It's not, "Is Nicole okay?" but more like, "I heard that Nicole blah-blah." There are a handful of girls who are the subject of every joke,' she continued, meaning herself.

Paris intimated that this manipulation by the media and friends with an agenda was a big part of the reason for their fall-out. 'There was no reason why we were fighting; it was just silly. We believed what other people were saying. People are really two-faced in this town, and they were trying to play us against each other. It made me sadder than any break-up with a boyfriend. It was just like the worst feeling ever,' she said, suggesting that it had all been for nothing.

The realisation that some people just weren't good for her didn't only extend to so-called friends and paparazzi. Over the last year, she had come to see that Rachel Zoe, her stylist, had gone too far. Quite what caused this fallout isn't entirely clear; in reality, it was probably a combination of factors. One, perhaps, was Nicole's weight.

As one paper commented on Zoe, 'Her look concentrates on oversized accessories – large bags to make arms look frail, men's watches to make wrists appear twig-like and sunglasses which render the face almost shrunken. The LA Times once claimed: "Fashion insiders have whispered privately that Zoe is single-handedly bringing back anorexia." The fad was not so very different from the heroin-chic look of the early 90s, which saw the waif-like, strung-out look shoot to meteoric popularity. (And, as with the anorexic look, heroin chic abruptly fell from grace after the high profile deaths of models and actresses.) For someone like Nicole, recovering from anorexia, spending time with Zoe was like an alcoholic spending time with a bartender. It was never going to end well. Nicole once commented that she wanted to surround herself with positive people and influences – the clear implication being that Zoe was emphatically not one of these.

The fall-out became more public after a message appeared on Nicole's MySpace page: 'What 35-year-old raisin-face whispers her order of three pieces of asparagus for dinner at Chateau every night, and hides her deathly disorder by pointing the finger at me, and used her last paycheck I wrote her to pay for a publicist instead of a nutritionist? HINT: Her nickname is Lettucecup.' Lindsay Lohan – a close friend of Nicole's and someone who had also hired Zoe to choose her clothes – replied with a smiley and the words, 'Hmmm... no comment.' It was, to anyone who knew the situation (and that included plenty of celebrities and Hollywood's rich and powerful) very obvious who and what it was all about.

Nicole denied posting the message, saying she never went on MySpace. 'My friend did it as a joke. When I saw it, I told them to take it down. I knew it wasn't the right thing to do.' Nevertheless, it had made the designer a laughing stock.

Nicole could hardly deny the truth of the content of the message, even if she didn't write it herself. Aside from the eating-disorder jibe, there was the odd sense that the designer had overreached herself, both professionally and personally. Zoe's increasing fame – or notoriety – had led her to publicise herself in a way that others thought strange, and perhaps even narcissistic. 'I've never met another stylist who has a publicist and an agent,' commented Nicole. The self-promotion spilled over into their personal relationship, with Zoe allegedly taking credit for Nicole's choices. Although Zoe had certainly had her input and taught Nicole a lot – giving her the tools to be her own stylist, in effect – Nicole protested, 'there's definitely an idea that Rachel styled me and she dressed me every day, like I was her Barbie.' (Barbie was, in fact, a pet name that Zoe gave to Nicole.) 'That's not the case. She dressed me for events.' The backlash was fierce, and included many of the 'Zoe-bots'. Nicole ended up hiring Cristina Ehrlich as a stylist, famous for working with Jessica Biel and Penelope Cruz.

Now that *The Simple Life* had finished, and life would be slowing down in the run up to the birth, Nicole had a chance to rethink what she wanted to be doing. The TV show had been great but, she realised – along with many more vocal critics – it had made her famous simply for being famous. There was nothing of substance in it. 'You know what?' she told Harper's Bazaar, 'I even said to Paris the other day, "I feel like I'm getting sick of us," and she said, "I do, too!"'

Her fashion work was important to her ('I'm the girl who loves photo shoots... I'll do photo shoots all day long...'), though there would be changes to come as her figure ballooned. Having said that, although the photo shoots would be different, Nicole didn't change her own style through her pregnancy. 'It's not like I blew up overnight. It gradually happened. When my jeans stopped fitting I wore the Balenciaga riding pants.' Nicole is a huge fan of Balenciaga. 'I like to be comfortable,' she said – though fortunately, that didn't mean she had to give up much. 'Luckily for me, I'm completely comfortable in six-inch heels.'

Her style may not have changed, but her weight and shape did. 'Half my wardrobe is already stretched... Not all my clothes fit the same. I don't even think it's a weight thing; I think your body just changes after you have a baby. I don't care either way,' she claimed, 'but I'm not used to having a tank top or bra underneath my clothes. You always hear that people with blond hair or larger breasts get more attention, but I never really thought that was real! I like wearing shirts that are a bit see-through because before it didn't really matter. But now it's like, "Uh-oh, I could get arrested!"'

Later in 2007, she went back to work on the album that had been postponed for so long thanks to *The Simple Life*, and was also working to finish a book about her style. Alongside that, she was launching a line of accessories based on some of her favourites: jewellery, scarves and the sunglasses for which she was famous. Eventually, she said, she would like to start her own label. Plus, she was working on a follow up to her semi-autobiographical novel, *The Truth About Diamonds*.

As if that wasn't enough, she and Madden had decided to start a new charity in LA. The idea was to help disadvantaged children – in America and worldwide. 'We grew up in Los Angeles and we want our child to be a part of the community, and to know that there's a responsibility to help the community,' she was quoted by *People magazine*. 'We named it the Richie Madden Children's Foundation because we each have families and our families are close, and our family is involved.'

The idea came to her after the couple received a mountain of baby equipment from family and friends, who obviously hadn't co-ordinated their efforts. 'I got like 10 cribs and 20 strollers. For one little girl! So we wanted to take the gifts we got and give them to the people who actually needed them.' A meeting with the charity advisory firm Inspired Philanthropy gave them some direction.

The two kick-started their charitable efforts by giving a surprise baby shower in November at a clinic in LA, in which they gave away almost $200,000-worth of presents to 100 mothers-to-be. 'We're lucky that we have families that get along and love each other,' commented Madden. 'I think it's great that our child will grow up as a part of that family. Sometimes people don't want to believe that me and Nicole are just a young couple having a baby and we're really excited. We don't really get to share our lives with people. It's nice to connect with people on a real level.'

Although most of the toys, cribs and clothes they gave away were for boys, the couple did not know the sex of their own baby. This was Madden's choice, and he had to work hard to keep it that way. 'I like to know everything,' Nicole said. 'If he wasn't at every doctor's appointment, I probably would have found out by now just behind his back and not told him.' She also suggested that, although they would consider marriage, that was not going to happen any time soon. 'I got to hold something for when I get older. I can't have everything happen in one year,' she explained.

Looming parenthood was also an opportunity to re-evaluate her relationship to her own parents. 'When I found out that I was pregnant, there was just something inside of me that felt a responsibility to mend any issues that I've had with my parents in the past, because, listen, I've put them through a lot,' People quoted her – adding that this meant her biological mother, not the adoptive mother she had spent most of her life with. She also tried to spend quality time with her boyfriend's mother. Her relationship with Lionel was better (thanks in part to the work they had done in therapy) and he was just thrilled to be a grandfather – though, he specified, he didn't want to be called 'grandpa'. He also recognised that she would now have a better insight into his and Brenda's actions when she was growing up. 'Motherhood has given her all the keys to understanding how her mother and I were trying to raise her. Now it has come full circle.' He also counselled her not to worry about what she would do next; it was ok to take a break from work. 'Especially in the case of Nicole, it's not only her dad and mom involved, but half of the world,' explained Lionel. 'So it's a bit of a challenge. So I told her, "Just enjoy the ride and take your time. Whatever you want to do, just make sure it's the right decision, make the decision and roll with it." If that does happen, you have a husband now and you have a baby now, so whenever that goes, it's going to be wonderful.'

On January 11, 2008, she gave birth to her first child at the Cedars Sinai Medical Centre, where she had previously had tests to diagnose her weight problem. They named the girl Harlow Winter Kate Madden. 'We are very blessed she's healthy and beautiful and so good already,' Madden told People. 'We are very happy.'

One thing that surprised Nicole was how much she enjoyed motherhood. 'Everybody talks about how difficult it is in the first three months, but I absolutely love it,' she said. One of her close friends agreed, 'Nicole is one of the most loving and nurturing mothers I have yet to come across.' Amazingly, for some who had known her in her pre-maternal life, plenty of others agreed. In the May after she gave birth, *Babytalk Magazine* announced that they were giving her the Golden Pacifier parenting award.

*Nicole Richie and Joel Madden take baby Harlow out for a
walk in Glendale, California, America - 21 May 2008*

In an interview with OK!, the magazine's chief editor, alluded to her wayward past but pointed out that things had changed a lot since she had had Harlow. 'Honouring Nicole Richie with a Babytalk Golden Pacifier Award might come as a surprise to some, but we felt that she deserved some recognition for her turnaround since becoming a mom. She's grown up a lot since the arrival of little Harlow, and her creation of the Richie-Madden Children's Foundation has demonstrated her efforts to set a good example by shining a spotlight on important issues affecting today's families.'

Motherhood meant a new stage in Nicole's life – not just in terms of the nights and nappy changes, but in terms of what it meant for her career. It was a new kind of publicity, and actually one that was quite positive for her. Some of this was down to the inevitable changes in behaviour that being a mother brought with it – although the press still had a field day when she and Madden left their new daughter in the care of a babysitter for a few hours one evening to go to an awards ceremony. It was the night of the Grammy's only a month or so after Harlow had been born. 'You know what,' she complained, 'I was gone for maybe three hours. I never go out. I go four or five days without leaving my house. But the press just went wild with it.' As time went on, she and Madden managed to get out once a week or so, perhaps to a movie – 'if the running time's not too long.'

But it also allowed the press to see a new side of her. Harper's Bazaar noted that, whereas celebrity gossip sites used to take pleasure in gleefully commenting on pictures of her looking skeletally thin in a bikini, now they were full of praise for her image, as well as plugging her new fashion lines – which included a jewellery line with Mouawad and a maternity collection. As she said in one interview, 'I owe the baby my life.'

Naturally there were publicity downsides, as well. The paparazzi were keen to get early shots of the new family, to the point where they would be disturbed by helicopters hovering over their house. They got around that problem by hanging a large swathe of webbing at the back of the house so that the cameras couldn't see what was going on underneath. Nicole commented how Sean Penn had done something similar. 'Didn't he write in rocks, like, "Fuck you" or something?' The net came down when Harlow was two.

In the meantime, she had gone public with some official pictures in *People magazine*. This was a compromise on her part; although Nicole tries to keep her private life – at least, the part of it that concerns her nearest and dearest – secret from the tabloids and magazines, she knew that secrecy just brought them out in droves. 'The day before it came out, I was nervous, because there was going to be a picture of my daughter everywhere,' she said. 'But if I didn't put a picture out, it would have been ten times worse. I wanted to stop people trying to get pictures of her. I was just being a protective mom.'

Nicole had already said how being a mother herself had brought her closer to her parents, and she found that Madden was seamlessly accepted into the Richie family. From some perspectives, this was strange, since he and Lionel Richie seem very different people. After all, she admitted that she and her boyfriend were very different – though it didn't seem to cause problems with them. 'Yeah, for being so opposite, we could possibly hate each other...'

Instead, she says, 'he has a different way of thinking. But at the same time, he's never tried to change me. And if anything, we were friends first. We just have fun together. When we're apart, we just get on iChat and don't even say anything to each other. He likes to get girly sometimes. But he'd kill me if he knew I said that!' Joel comes from a large family, something Nicole has said she would like to replicate for herself.

Richie senior also noted 'He has a solid value system.' He and Lionel turned out to have a lot in common. Nicole introduced him to her parents early on in the relationship. 'I brought him over to my dad's house. They're both musicians, they're both from the South, and they're both very conservative, so they got along right away. My dad really respects Joel as an artist, and they're both really great songwriters.'

And, of course, they had Nicole in common; it was hard to tell who was her biggest fan. Lionel explained the public interest in her this way: 'It's because she is real. She is always brutally honest. What she says is what she means. Everywhere I go, they love Nicole. She would be a hit anywhere. I love her so much, and that's not speaking as her father, that's speaking as a fan.'

Three months after Harlow was born, Madden took her on a surprise holiday to the California desert for the Coachella Valley Music and Arts Festival. 'She hasn't been able to do a whole lot over the year, so we're having a little family trip,' he told People. 'I rented a house and surprised Nicole with a weekend trip because she likes Coachella. She was like, "I really want to go!" So I surprised her. We brought the baby.' Paris Hilton also went to the festival, along with her boyfriend – Joel Madden's brother, Benji. (Asked whether she thought Paris would be the next mother in her group of friends, she answered, 'Ha, no – but I don't think anyone would have bet on me.') Paris was almost as excited about Harlow as Nicole was, being a sort of aunt to her friend's baby. 'I'm so excited! I've sent her all these presents. I'm going to spoil her!' US magazine quoted her. She added that she thought 'Harlow Madden' was the 'coolest name ever,' intimating that it was a little surprising that Nicole had managed to come up with something like that. 'I'm like, "That is the coolest name, oh my God!" I wouldn't even think she would have thought of that. It's a beautiful name. Nicole is so into it. She always knows what's cool before it happens,' she conceded.

The trip away to the festival was clearly a big deal for Nicole, prompting her to comment on how much her priorities had changed over the course of the last year – bearing in mind that just a year earlier, in the first days of her pregnancy, she was looking at a spell in jail and rehab for her second DUI offence. 'You know, I went through a stage of thinking that once you had a baby, you moved to Brentwood, had a white picket fence, and it changed your entire life,' she said. 'But I love where I am right now. Every single thing is for Harlow. Joel took me out last week, and he was like, "Why don't we go out and have a shopping day?" But I ended up only going to kid stores. I didn't get to buy shoes or anything.'

In the same interview the couple spoke about the ups and downs of living in LA. Madden clearly didn't like the paparazzi activity, and had voiced ideas about buying a place in Sydney or Thailand, a bolt-hole to avoid them when it all got too much – not to mention its effects on their baby. Nicole, on the other hand, wasn't so sure – perhaps because the paparazzi were more central to her way of life, in that she was a bigger part of the celebrity culture that had lifted her to fame. 'I personally love Los Angeles,' she said. 'You can say anything you want about L.A., but kids get into things. I know that I grew up on the faster side, but I don't think that a town matters if you know who you are.' They did buy an apartment in New York, which is a bit slower-paced – especially in terms of the paparazzi.

Her easier pace of life and the constraints of parenthood didn't mean she was stuck at home writing books and designing clothes all the time. She was trying to expand her repertoire, moving into acting. Other than *The Simple Life*, her TV roles had been restricted to interviews and the occasional part here and there, such as her role in 2005's *American Dreams*. In 2008, however, she won a part in the NBC spy comedy-drama, *Chuck*, in which a computer geek is unwittingly drawn into the world of espionage. She would be playing Heather Chandler, the unkind schoolgirl enemy of the protagonist. 'Nicole auditioned for the part and was very funny,' the executive producer, Josh Schwartz, commented. 'This role is a great opportunity for her to show off her comedic skills and be diabolically evil and kick some butt. It's going to be really fun.'

She was also considering the idea of working on a musical; there were rumours early in 2008 that she would be appearing in Chicago. US magazine reported, 'Nicole Richie has been offered the lead role of Roxie Hart in the Broadway production of Chicago, US Weekly reports exclusively in its latest issue, on newsstands now. Richie, 26, who welcomed daughter Harlow with Joel Madden on Jan. 12, is undecided. "She's definitely interested and weighing it out with the timing of the baby," a Richie pal tells US. "It is in the super early stages of discussions and no decision has been made yet. It would give her a reason to really show her talent and to stay in the new place in NY Joel just got... It also shows people are really excited about Nicole right now.'

Nicole wasn't as enthusiastic as the 'source', noting that a six-week-old baby wasn't conducive to late nights and high-kicking on Broadway. 'Doing musical theater really does take up your entire life. But I'm really excited to get out there and show people that I'm capable of doing something other than *The Simple Life*.'

At the end of 2008, less than a year after she had given birth to Harlow, Nicole fell pregnant again. In February 2009, Madden wrote a message entitled 'Better than winning as OSCAR' on the Good Charlotte site: 'I am so happy to tell everyone that Harlow is going to be a big sister! God has truly blessed my family. Hope you're all feeling as good as i am right now.'

This time, she didn't take much of a break. She had a number of different fashion projects lined up and made sure she followed them through before she gave birth in September. Appropriately enough, now that she was a celebrity mother, one of her most high-profile projects was a collection for A Pea in the Pod, the brand of stylish maternity wear. 'I'm excited to join A Pea in the Pod in creating my capsule collection,' she stated in a press release. 'I hope that the ease and comfort of my designs will help expectant moms to look and feel amazing throughout their pregnancy.'

'The 14-piece capsule collection captures

Nicole Richie's signature bohemian look with key items such as the peasant top, caftan, cascade cardigan, patio dress, and maxi skirt,' read another statement. 'Signature details like asymmetric hems, braid trim and smocking are important elements in this free-spirited collection. Tissue knits and silk are available at prices that range from a $48 tank top to a $148 maxi dress.' The release date was August 7, 2009 – just too late to enjoy for her own pregnancy.

'Working with Nicole was a great experience,' enthused Rebecca Matthias, the company's President and Chief Creative Officer. 'Her style exudes a natural, effortless beauty, and there is nothing more natural and beautiful than a pregnant woman's glow.'

At the end of 2008 she had finally released her jewellery collection, a collaboration with Mouawad entitled House of Harlow 1960, after her daughter. The line turned out to be extremely popular – selling out online before it even reached the shelves – and has been worn by many celebrities, including Madonna and Ashlee Simpson. As suggested by the name, it was inspired by Nicole's love of the 60s. 'The collection is targeted at girls in their teens to women in their 30s who admire her and the prices range from $30 to $150,' ran the PR. The designs featured 'fabric, leather, silk strings, chains, rivets, feathers and gold-plated metals.'

She was also bringing out a new line of footwear to complement the Mouawad collection. Nicole was planning to add around 20 styles of shoe as well as belts, bags and accessories. 'Nicole is designing everything herself,' her business partner, Rick Cytrynbaum, told *Contactmusic*. 'She's totally devoted to this, and we're creating a whole lifestyle around her aesthetic and what is true to her.' The interest proved that, although Nicole might once have needed Rachel Zoe to give her fashion tips, she had indeed long since outgrown the size-zero stylist's help.

With her fashion line taking off, it was only natural that she would be asked to act as a judge on Season 7 of Project Runway, casting for which began in May 2009. The reality show is hosted by Heidi Klum and sees contestants competing to create clothes within time, budget and other constraints. 'Nicole is a fabulous guest judge,' Sara Rea, Runway's executive producer, told People. 'She has strong opinions and gives clear and specific constructive criticism to the designers. Also, she isn't afraid to disagree with the other judges.' Previous judges had included Christina Aguilera, Eva Longoria Parker, Lindsay Lohan and Cindy Crawford.

Versatility is the name of Nicole's game, and with a musical background and family – Richie senior as well as her partner Madden – she decided once again to try out that string to her bow. She formed a rock band called Darling with model and actress Josie Maran, though it turned out that this would only be on a casual basis – between motherhood and her other work, she didn't have a lot of time to advance that career at this point. Amid speculation she was making an album, she told People, 'I do eventually want to record an album, but right now I have a lot on my plate. I've really been working hard – going on auditions for acting, doing design for my line, and being a mom – so that pretty much takes up my days. Right now I'm reading scripts and really trying to take my work seriously.'

Along with these more commercial projects, she was expanding her charity work too. In recent years, she had become more aware of the human rights abuses that were occurring in parts of Africa, as the trade in valuable minerals intersects with corrupt regimes who control them, and use them to fund their operations. A growing number of celebrities were raising awareness, knowing that consumer goods in the West are often manufactured using raw materials mined from these areas. The area that caught Nicole's attention was the Congo. Ignored by the news for years (some say because the government has no oil interest there) the plight of the Congo's women has come to the fore in recent times.

'I am about to tell you a story about a place where babies and grandmothers are being raped on a daily basis and the reason they are being raped is directly connected to the purchases of our cell phones, of our laptops and of our ipods,' she stated in a video published by the Mirror online. Congo suffers from one of the highest rates of sexual violence in the world, with rape used as a weapon of war and to control the valuable 'conflict minerals'. Since the destination of so many of these minerals is ultimately the US, this is an issue she found it hard to dodge. Other celebrities who had picked up the cause include George Clooney,

Matt Damon, Angelina Jolie and Brad Pitt.

In June, she had a piece of unexpected bad news – as did millions of fans all over the world. Michael Jackson, the so-called King of Pop, and Nicole's godfather, died in mysterious circumstances on 25th June, aged 50.

The Twittersphere was lit up with messages from celebrities as well as fans. Paris Hilton posted a photo of herself, her sister and Nicole with Jackson, with the text: 'I'm still in shock about Michael. My mom grew up with him since they were teenagers and I've known him all my life. He was amazing, so sad. Michael and his kids were just at my house a few months ago, I can't believe I will never see him again. He was such a kind and gentle soul.'

Nicole herself stayed silent about it, but Madden posted, 'I'm getting off the computer. Gonna spend time with my family. It was a sad day. Need a break from all of this. Rest in Peace Michael.'

Later, rumours would circulate that Nicole planned to name her next child after her godfather – Michael if he was a boy, Michelle if it was a girl. 'Nicole is devastated by Michael's death. She loved him and it happened so suddenly. She wasn't planning on naming the baby after him but she thinks it's fitting now that he's gone,' a 'source' supposedly told one magazine. In the event, it didn't happen, which casts doubt on the source's accuracy, or existence.

The baby was born on September 9, 2009 – a boy. The couple named their baby Sparrow James Midnight Madden. 'In the middle of night, the very early hours of September 9, 2009, Sparrow James Midnight Madden was born to Nicole Richie and Joel Madden,' they posted on her website. 'He weighs 7lbs 14oz. Nicole, Joel, Harlow and Sparrow are all doing well. Thank you for all of your good wishes.'

Six weeks later they followed the same pattern that they had with Harlow and ran a piece with *People magazine*, again hoping to short-circuit some of the media circus that surrounded her personal life. 'I couldn't be happier,' she told them. 'The only thing you want is for your kids to be healthy and happy, and they are. I'm right where I belong.' Harlow, she said, was living up to her job as big sister. 'She's very gentle with him,' Madden said. 'I'm glad I had a girl before I had a boy,' Nicole agreed. 'She just loves him so much.'

A few months later in February 2010, rumours started to circulate about her engagement with Madden. They originally announced it in an interview for The Late Show with David Letterman, but although there were only four days in between taping and airing the show, Madden let the cat out of the bag – once again via Twitter. 'Yep. I'm engaged. Very happy. Yeah we've been engaged for a while so you're all kinds of late on that. But Thanks for the hooplah all the same.' It turned out that he had proposed at least two months earlier, at the end of 2009. He thanked his family and friends for keeping it a secret. Later that night, however, he realised his mistake and deleted the posts – too late, since enough people had seen them and copied them by that point. The next morning, he wrote, 'Just woke up. I'm screwed. Oh boy.'

The plan was to marry at a spa resort in California in the Autumn. They hired Mindy Weiss to plan the wedding; Weiss has previously managed celebrity weddings for stars including for Pete Wentz and Ashlee Simpson. There was one detail that Weiss wouldn't get a look in on – the dress. Nicole would be designing this herself. 'She wants something loose and not too formal because her kids are going to be in the wedding. They're a handful!' a source stated.

Again, the veracity of the source was called into question when subsequent reports from Nicole herself suggested that she hadn't even started planning it yet – something she was claiming as late as June. Shortly afterwards, reports surfaced – again from anonymous 'sources' – that the wedding was off. The Daily News quoted an 'insider', 'Their wedding is off for now. Nicole is upset that Joel seems more interested in being on the road with his buddies, boozing and hanging out in bars than he is in sharing family time in LA. It's become a joke among Nicole's family and friends how many times she's planned and postponed the ceremony.' In the absence of any hard facts, rumours like this always circulate in Hollywood circles; if a quote from the celeb in question is not forthcoming, hearsay will do so long as it is interesting enough to sell a few copies of the magazine or score a few hits on a website.

At the end of June, Nicole did make an announcement, but it was about her new book, not her wedding. 'I'm proud to finally announce that my second novel Priceless will be out this fall on September 28th, 2010,' she wrote on her blog. 'This book has been a project that I've put my heart and soul into and I'm happy that I get to share it with you here first. Hope you enjoy it.'

She was also busy helping her close friend, Lindsay Lohan, who had become the most recent of their group to face a jail term for a DUI offence; Lohan had been sentenced to 90 days for violating the terms of her probation for an offence committed in 2007. Having said that, experts were predicting that she would spend only a week or so inside, in the same way that Nicole had been let off lightly.

Bing Hosts A Celebration of Creative Minds, Los Angeles, America - 22 Jun 2010

Conclusion

Nicole has certainly crammed a lot into her life, particularly over the last seven years, when she has been the subject of such media attention.

There have been highs and lows, but the running theme is that it is all captured for posterity and broadcast to her adoring public, who devour any and all news about her. In that respect, she is the most modern of celebrities: famous for being famous, then for getting it wrong, and finally for getting it right – the classic rags-to-riches tale, with a few kinks along the way for the sake of interest.

More recently, there have been some efforts to censor some of the more colourful episodes from her past, and rewrite history to some extent. As a mother of two, and an increasingly respectable fashion designer, Nicole's image is shifting away from that of the wild girl who, at one stage in her life, was staying up partying all night and meeting drug dealers in some of LA's less reputable car parks in the small hours of the morning. But of course, the chat shows and tabloids all still love to talk about those days – they're part of the reason she is famous in the first place. And that doesn't always go down too well. In June 2010, she was due to appear on the *Today Show* in Australia. Her fee for the appearance was a cool £117,000, and a goody-bag of extras worth £17,500 was thrown in too. With expenses, the total bill came to £175,000 for the three days. Surely they could expect some good material for that? Her publicist had other ideas. As an advert for the show ran a few minutes before starting the live interview, referencing some of the interesting ways Nicole had caught the public's attention in the past, the Mail reports that she flew into a rage, forbidding all mention of these subjects. An insider reported, 'We ran the teaser for the interview explaining Nicole Richie's background and the various ways she came to fame, but her publicist hit the roof and started yelling at the crew that those subjects couldn't be covered.'

Lisa Wilkinson, the host for Today, was told in no uncertain terms about what she could and couldn't ask Nicole. 'Her publicist continued to carry on off-camera... No one on the show had ever seen anything like it.'

It's only natural that Nicole would want the press and public to move on from those days, but it's also natural that they keep asking her about them. After all, they are an important part of her past, and one of the things that people love about her is that she has overcome so many different forms of adversity – parents separating, drugs, alcohol, criminal charges, eating disorders, a feud with her best friend, and all under the watchful eye of the cameras. And even those closest to her reference these things from time to time, albeit a little more sensitively.

Accepting an Icon award at the TV Land Awards, Lionel Richie commented on his daughter, 'Forget about surviving 40 years in the music business. Just surviving 27 years of Nicole Richie has been a struggle-and-a-half, I want to tell you. I stand here as a survivor, I want you to know, for all the parents out there.'

According to Richie senior, Nicole has 'made some mistakes in her life'. However, he brought her up to take responsibility for what she did. 'She has not blamed others for her problems and is growing up very quickly, albeit in the heat of the media spotlight,' Lionel told US magazine.

'My father taught me to stand straight and take whatever punishment or hardships were the result of my own actions, and I am proud that I was able to hand that philosophy down to my daughter.'

And, of course, these problems keep recurring. Not that she has been arrested in a while – motherhood does seem to have changed her, almost beyond recognition. But the legal consequences of her actions continue. In June 2010, her probation was extended by a year to March 2011, because she had missed some of her alcohol education classes – a condition of probation from her arrest in 2006 – to look after her children. The past has long arms, and none more so than for Nicole – though it's clear that she too wants to leave it behind. 'I live my life and I do what I do, and sometimes you forget that people are watching you,' she told Marie Claire recently. 'Look, people can give reason after reason. To me, I've just accepted responsibility for what I've done, and I don't really try and look at why I did it. I just feel that I have gotten past it and moved on, and it's just something that's not really a part of my life any more. And I feel extremely blessed to live the life that I'm living.'

'You know,' she continued, 'I'm just one to live in the present and enjoy the time that I'm having. Going back into my past is just not something that I do. Right now, I'm living my dreams.' That sounds like an accurate assessment. 2010 is looking like a big year for Nicole. There is – possibly – her wedding to look forward to. Her fashion career is also continuing to move forwards with increasing pace; she visited the Glamour Woman of the Year awards in London in June ('My fake british accent is in full effect tonight!' she tweeted), picking up the Entrepreneur of the Year award for the House of Harlow 1960 brand. Given that her partying days seem to be over, it's likely that she will continue pushing that side of her life as she settles down to the roles of wife and mother.

Whatever she decides to do, though, or whatever life brings, Nicole is someone who will always be in the spotlight. She seems to be able to overcome problems and turn them to her advantage, possessing a talent for engaging the public and keeping them coming back for more.

We'll see a lot more of that in the years to come.